Understanding Success and Failure in Adult ESL

NEW PERSPECTIVES ON LANGUAGE AND EDUCATION

Founding Editor: Viv Edwards, *University of Reading, UK*
Series Editors: Phan Le Ha, *University of Hawaii at Manoa, USA* **and**
Joel Windle, *Monash University, Australia.*

Two decades of research and development in language and literacy education have yielded a broad, multidisciplinary focus. Yet education systems face constant economic and technological change, with attendant issues of identity and power, community and culture. What are the implications for language education of new 'semiotic economies' and communications technologies? Of complex blendings of cultural and linguistic diversity in communities and institutions? Of new cultural, regional and national identities and practices? The New Perspectives on Language and Education series will feature critical and interpretive, disciplinary and multidisciplinary perspectives on teaching and learning, language and literacy in new times. New proposals, particularly for edited volumes, are expected to acknowledge and include perspectives from the Global South. Contributions from scholars from the Global South will be particularly sought out and welcomed, as well as those from marginalized communities within the Global North.

All books in this series are externally peer-reviewed.

Full details of all the books in this series and of all our other publications can be found on http://www.multilingual-matters.com, or by writing to Multilingual Matters, St Nicholas House, 31-34 High Street, Bristol, BS1 2AW, UK.

NEW PERSPECTIVES ON LANGUAGE AND EDUCATION: 106

Understanding Success and Failure in Adult ESL

Superación vs Dropout of Adult English Learners in the US

Taewoong Kim

MULTILINGUAL MATTERS
Bristol • Jackson

DOI https://doi.org/10.21832/KIM2408
Library of Congress Cataloging in Publication Data
A catalog record for this book is available from the Library of Congress.
Names: Kim, Taewoong, - author.
Title: Understanding Success and Failure in Adult ESL: Superación vs Dropout of
   Adult English Learners in the US / Taewoong Kim.
Description: Bristol; Jackson: Multilingual Matters, [2022] | Series: New
   Perspectives on Language and Education: 106 | Includes bibliographical
   references and index. | Summary: "This book explores the reasons why adult
   ESL learners drop out of their language classes and suggests explicit strategies for
   keeping students engaged. The most effective strategies may be personal rather
   than technical or curricular"—Provided by publisher.
Identifiers: LCCN 2021057233 (print) | LCCN 2021057234 (ebook) | ISBN
   9781800412392 (Paperback) | ISBN 9781800412408 (Hardback) | ISBN
   9781800412415 (Adobe PDF) | ISBN 9781800412422 (ePub)
Subjects: LCSH: English language—Study and teaching—United States. | English
   language—Study and teaching—Spanish speakers.
Classification: LCC PE1068.U5 K46 2022 (print) | LCC PE1068.U5 (ebook) | DDC
   428.0071/5—dc23/eng/20220202
LC record available at https://lccn.loc.gov/2021057233
LC ebook record available at https://lccn.loc.gov/2021057234

British Library Cataloguing in Publication Data
A catalogue entry for this book is available from the British Library.

ISBN-13: 978-1-80041-240-8 (hbk)
ISBN-13: 978-1-80041-239-2 (pbk)

Multilingual Matters
UK: St Nicholas House, 31-34 High Street, Bristol, BS1 2AW, UK.
USA: Ingram, Jackson, TN, USA.

Website: www.multilingual-matters.com
Twitter: Multi_Ling_Mat
Facebook: https://www.facebook.com/multilingualmatters
Blog: www.channelviewpublications.wordpress.com

The policy of Multilingual Matters/Channel View Publications is to use papers
that are natural, renewable and recyclable products, made from wood grown in
sustainable forests. In the manufacturing process of our books, and to further
support our policy, preference is given to printers that have FSC and PEFC Chain
of Custody certification. The FSC and/or PEFC logos will appear on those books
where full certification has been granted to the printer concerned.

Typeset by Deanta Global Publishing Services, Chennai, India.

Contents

Acknowledgements

I want to thank many people who have supported the birth of this book. I sincerely thank my wife Hyojung Park, and my sons Leo Yoon Kim and Philip Geon Kim for their support despite the unusual COVID-19 pandemic situation. Also, I thank Lawrence Baines for inspiring me to keep going forward, and Lauren Albin, Georgeanne Yehling, Myoyoung Kim, Ji Hong, Kyungsook Yeum and Daniel Rueckert for their tremendous help and insightful feedback on the early drafts of this book. I thank Anna Roderick and the Multilingual Matters team for their considerate support. Last but not least, I want to thank the six participants of this book and their families for letting their voices heard. Without their dedication, this book would not have been possible.

Taewoong Kim

Preface

In recent years, the California wildfires have killed over a hundred people, and more than a quarter of a million Californians have been evacuated from their houses. However, in the midst of this conflagration, Latino migrant workers have continued to pick berries and grapes all day and night despite the fire, smoke and danger, because evacuation announcements are often delivered only in English (Barry-Jester, 2019; Sesin, 2017).

In the US, almost one in five workers, about 28 million people, are immigrants (US Department of Labor, 2021). Of these 28 million, only 3% have ever enrolled in English classes (US Department of Education, Office of Career, Technical, and Adult Education, 2019). Despite adult English learners' (ELs) natural inclination to learn English, they often drop out of their classes without saying a word. Lacking the resources to research what made their students' drop out, teachers often attribute their absence to mysterious forces at home or work. About learning English, Juan (pseudonym), one of my adult students told me, 'I want to learn English, but I learn nothing. The teachers care about the money, not us. They just talk, talk, talk. No learning'.

Through a qualitative study, this book explores what makes adult Spanish-speaking ELs stay or drop out of English class. The findings reveal that adult ELs' decision to stay or drop out is complex, multifaceted and dynamic. Superación, a Spanish word meaning self-improvement and self-actualization, was central to adult ELs' decision to invest in learning English. ELs' multifaceted sociocultural backgrounds, needs and factors for investing in learning English were found to be dynamic and fluid, consisting of both cognitive and affective aspects. When students felt that a teacher genuinely cared, when they could see visible evidence that they were learning the language, when teachers were engaging and responsive, they experienced superación. Without superación, students dropped out.

This book tells the untold stories of and gives voice to adult ELs in a community English literacy class through three questions: Who are they? What makes them invest in learning English? and What makes them quit? The journey to hear their voices began one night when my car was broken into at the class parking lot. Details of that night are provided in the Introduction.

Introduction: A Broken Car

It was 8pm and the sky was pitch black. The church classroom where I taught English as a second language (ESL) to adults in Oklahoma City was empty as the students had all gone home. Mine was the lone car in the parking lot and my engine refused to start.

Suddenly, I remembered a colleague's comments, 'John (I go by 'John' as my English nickname), please be careful where you teach. That area has one of the highest crime rates in the state'. But I was stuck and alone in an empty parking lot. In the darkness, using my iPhone's flashlight, I looked at the class roster. There was a student named Domingo (pseudonym) who always participated and seemed like a nice guy.

'Hola', Domingo answered.

'Hello Domingo, this is John Kim, your teacher', I said.

Domingo showed up at the parking lot 10 minutes later.

He opened the hood and looked at the engine.

'Any wrong sound?' Domingo asked.

'Phu-shu, phu-she, phu-shu sounds when I stop my car', I replied.

'Hmm, it might be the gas pump, I'll call a friend'.

Domingo had a short conversation in Spanish over the phone with his friend. Domingo's friend, a car mechanic, said he would tow my car from the parking lot to his repair shop and I could pick it up tomorrow.

I asked, 'Would it be better to call my insurance company and have them tow my car? My insurance company can pay for the towing fee'.

Domingo said, 'Towing is free, he never charges for towing. He once towed my car for a long, long way for free. Besides, we are friends'.

I thought about being in the 'most dangerous area' and I did not really know Domingo all that well. I mean, he was a diligent student, but did I know him well enough to hand over the keys of my car?

On the other hand, he had dropped everything to come rescue his ESL teacher in the middle of the night.

'Okay, Domingo, thank you very much. So we can meet tomorrow at your friend's repair shop to pick up my car?'

'Yes'.

'Great, how much is the cost to repair?'

'Let's say 110 dollars'.

'Check or cash?'

'Cash', Domingo laughed.

So, we made a deal and Domingo gave me a ride back home, a 'side trip' for him of about 40 miles. In the car, we talked about that night's class material, which was about house layout with several vocabulary words such as patio, yard, bedroom, bathroom, living room and den.

To practice what we learned, I asked, 'How many bedrooms do you have? Do you have a patio in your house?'

'No, teacher, two bedroom, and no patio, no yard. I live in a trailer'.

The following morning, a friend drove me to the repair shop in downtown. The closer I got, the more uneasy I felt. The repair shop was very close to big homeless shelters in a shabby part of downtown. The shops around the repair shop had broken windows and no signs. The car 'repair shop' also had no signs, no windows and was actually an abandoned gas station. My car was among five or six others scattered around the lot.

When my friend and I got out of the car, Domingo just popped up out of nowhere.

'Hi teacher'.

We shook hands, and together looked at my car. My car's hood was covered with dusty fingerprints, hundreds of fingerprints everywhere.

'Spark plugs', Domingo said.

Domingo jumped in the car, and it started right away.

I gave him $110 in cash and thanked him profusely for rescuing me and fixing my car.

So, this is what I learned about Domingo. He lives in a trailer and his friend the mechanic works out of an abandoned gas station and accepts cash only. Over the course of only two days, I learned more about my adult ESL students than I had learned about them through the previous two semesters.

I have taught English to adult ESL learners for five years. In this particular center, I teach from August to December and January to May and typically have about 20 students, all of whom speak Spanish as their first language (L1).

In fall 2016, a health problem compelled me to take two months off. When I came back the following spring, only four students were left, and Domingo was one of them. I began this book because I wanted to understand why those 16 adult ESL learners stopped coming to class. I also wanted to know why those four students stayed.

1 Voices Unheard from the Margins

Thousands of adults come to English as a second language (ESL) classes with great hopes of mastering English. Many of them come in the evening after a long day of work, despite having families at home and untold chores to do (e.g. babysitting duties for friends and preparing cultural events such as the quinceañera [a Mexican cultural celebration of a girl's 15th birthday]). When an ESL student decides to leave, some administrators might think that the students 'were just too busy' or that 'they were not proficient enough to follow instructions' or even that 'they are not smart enough, they don't have a high school diploma'. However, adult learners, especially immigrants, are, by nature, problem-solvers (Vinogradov & Liden, 2009). Often, they work at several different jobs while living in a foreign country. They learn to adapt to the environment by learning how to support their family, raise their children and get along in their communities. They build up their own networks and establish intimate relationships to solve problems.

In the US, 17.4% of the labor force is foreign born. Most of these individuals have a mother tongue other than English (US Census Bureau, 2020). A fundamental challenge for immigrants living in the US is overcoming the barriers of limited English proficiency (Comings, 2007; Greenberg et al., 2001; Kim et al., 2011). For immigrants, learning English is paramount; a problem that must be solved to ensure survival. When an adult ESL student knocks on the door of a classroom, they are usually motivated and determined to succeed. Norton-Peirce (1995) called the learning of adult ESL students a way of *investing* in the future (Darvin & Norton, 2015; Norton-Peirce, 1995; Peirce, 2000). Most would do whatever it takes, regarding time, adjusting work schedules and negotiating family responsibilities so that they can learn English. According to Darvin and Norton's (2015) model of investment, taking ESL classes, *investing* for learning and staying in or dropping out are all human actions related to the sociocultural and historically situated meaning/identity construction processes.

On the first day of my teaching ESL at the Center for English Literacy (pseudonym) in fall 2016, only one student showed up. By Thanksgiving, enrollment had increased to 20 students. Most of the students were from Latin America, with Spanish as their mother tongue. The students worked as restaurant servers, factory workers, construction laborers and hotel housekeeping staff.

This book explores why adult ESL students drop out and why they stay. In order to explore reasons based on participants' real stories, I delved into the students' lives, not only inside the classroom, but also outside the classroom, because students, by nature, bring their learning interests from home to school and vice versa (Auerbach, 1993; Barth, 1972; Dewey, 1903; Krapp, 1999). Learning is an organic and dynamic activity, formed socioculturally in complex ways, predicated upon the adult students' motivation, which is both complex and multifaceted (Canagarajah, 2006; Norton-Peirce, 1995).

Adult ESL students who come to ESL classes expend significant time, energy and money. In 2016, the US Department of Labor reported that 51.9% of Latinx immigrants' jobs were hard labor, working mostly in the construction, housekeeping and manufacturing fields (US Department of Labor, 2017). Hard labor jobs are at the margins of our society and thus are the immigrant workers' lives. One of the core reasons that adult ESL learners learn English is that they view English as enabling them to move from the margins where they live to the central circle of society (Norton-Peirce, 1995; Wang, 2006). For example, immigrant adult ESL learners want to improve their English to work in better conditions such as working in an office, instead of working in the fields day and night (Kim, 2018). When the connection between what a student wants to learn and what is offered in terms of instruction is not apparent, the students' learning motivation may decrease (Comings, 2007; Han, 2009; Hidi *et al.*, 1992; Krapp, 1999). While retention is a hot topic for undergraduates in college and high school students (Jimerson *et al.*, 2002), it is also a critical factor when working with adult immigrant ESL students.

Adult English Learner Dropouts

What makes adult English learners (ELs) drop out despite the increasing numbers of ELs? The adult EL enrollment rate for adult English literacy classes has decreased over the last decade from 1.1 million (2005–2006) to 0.7 million (2015–2016) (Office of Career, Technical, and Adult Education, 2010, 2019). Research has investigated adult EL characteristics (Buttaro, 2002, 2004; Ellis, 2004; Gault, 2003; Gordon, 2004; McVay, 2004; Skilton-Sylvester, 2002), and some researchers have focused on adult learner's persistence (Comings, 2007; Kerka, 2005; New England Literacy Resource Center, 2009). However, the adult EL dropout phenomenon has gained relatively less scholarly attention nationwide compared to other populations such as high school or college students. The lack of English proficiency or fewer opportunities to improve their English proficiency among the adult immigrant EL population leads to unstable, fatalistic and hopeless attitudes toward English learning (Freire, 1996; Macedo, 2000). Therefore, it is necessary to understand the reasons for dropping out to more effectively and meaningfully support adult immigrant learners of English.

2 Theoretical Frameworks

In this chapter, I first review social justice through English language teaching (ELT) as the overarching framework of this study. Then, I review the spectrum of second language acquisition (SLA) studies and where this study's dominant theoretical framework, investment (Darvin & Norton, 2015), is located on the continuum. Following a detailed review of investment constructs, the dropout factors of push, pull and fall out (Doll *et al.*, 2013) are reviewed, as it is the second framework adapted in investigating what made the adult learners quit their investment. Lastly, I review the consideration of adult English learners' (ELs) situatedness (Lave & Wenger, 1991) and the holistic and ecological nature of SLA (Douglas Fir Group, 2016) to advocate for the necessity of a paradigm shift in second language (L2) teaching.

Social Justice through English Language Teaching

In the field of ELT, the topic of social justice emerged with the consideration of critical pedagogy and social transformation through education (Akbari, 2008; Hall, 2016; Hastings & Jacob, 2016). Social justice is defined as socially made conceptualizations, norms and practices toward what is right and what is wrong over time. The specific definition and intricacies of social justice are ever-evolving, dynamic and fluid, as reflected in the characteristics of its counterpart, social injustice, which has no end as it is culturally defined and perceived (Hall, 2016; McLaren, 2016).

Social justice: The conceptualization

The notion of social 'injustice' is a good starting point to consider what social justice refers to. Historically, it would be thought-provoking to note that missionary teachers in the 19th-century US actively saw themselves as 'helping' Native American students and taught them under the notion of 'social justice' at that time, in which they believed that 'Indians would ultimately confront a fateful choice: civilization or extinction' (Adams, 1995: 6). The concept of social justice for the missionary teachers during this time period was to 'civilize the Indians' from their 'savage lifestyle' by educating them through boarding school systems; in other words, by isolating and excluding the Native American students from what they viewed as 'uncivilized' life. In fact, this justification helped hide the brutal colonization of Native Americans behind the term 'civilizing'. A French writer of the era, Jules Ferry, even argued that 'the superior nations must civilize the inferior races' (Ennis, 1945: 326). Educators in the 21st century might argue that the 19th-century missionary teachers' beliefs and actions were too radical because they denigrated or subtracted the heritage of native peoples and violated their human rights to achieve their goals. However, the consensus in the 19th century was that civilizing supposedly 'savage people' was a form of social justice. The belief of equating 'civilization' and 'social justice' was destructive for the people who suffered from such 'justice'. In retrospect, perhaps it was most harmful for the identities of students (Norton-Peirce, 1995; Peirce, 2000). 'Taking out' an individual from his/her cultural heritage space is based on the rationale of an inferior–superior cultural dichotomy such as racism or neocolonialism, which is unjust (Patel, 2015). Being removed from one's heritage through subtractive schooling (Valenzuela, 2005) can dehumanize and harm one's identity. For this reason, considerations about 'humanity and identity' typically are at the center of discussions of social justice (Canagarajah, 2006; Hall, 2016; Nieto, 1994; Peirce, 2000).

Influences from biases to mind

Scholars have found that aspects of 'humanity and identity' can be influenced, either positively or negatively, by social justice issues:

- social/racial/gender/economic differences (Hall, 2016: 4);
- unequal power dynamics between social groups – oppressors vs. the oppressed (Freire, 1996, 1998);
- underlying and imposing mindsets through holistic socially made classes and structures (Bernstein, 1971; Macedo, 1994; Macedo & Bartolomé, 2014).

Exclusion from social resources, which include not only materialistic resources such as money, cars, houses or food, but also literacy and numeracy knowledge and skills, harms the people who are implicitly and explicitly oppressed (Freire, 1996; Peirce, 2000). Particularly for adult ELs, learning English is a fundamental resource.

Another example of social injustice would be the racism-based notions, norms and terminology in our society. Such terminologies implicitly convey racism in our daily lives toward certain groups of people, although the concept of 'race' is a social construct. For example, 'border-rats' was used to refer to Mexican-Americans living on the border (Macedo, 2000), sending a negative message and image of the 'race' to the public.

The hierarchical mentality provided through *terms, social norms* and *unearned privileges* schematizes a binary conceptualization about *what is right or standard* and *what is not standard, thus wrong*. In English as a second language (ESL) classrooms, the use of 'standard English' implies that it is the only 'legitimate' English to teach. Usually 'standard English' refers to White English speakers' English use, their pronunciation, ways of composing phrases and idioms (Chantrain, 2016). It seems clear that the well-known 'English-only policy' adopted by ESL institutions since the 1980s is based on the binary mindset of English as *right* and whole variant forms of English are *wrong*. Yet, research has found that encouraging ESL students to use their first language (L1) can bring positive effects to L2 learning (Auerbach, 1993; Storch & Wigglesworth, 2003). However, ESL teachers often seem to forbid their students from using their L1 for the sake of improving their L2 (Storch & Wigglesworth, 2003).

In the 21st-century ESL classroom, antagonism toward L1 use and variant forms of English still lingers. The term 'nativism' in ESL refers to biased racism in teaching. Nieto (1994) advocates for an awareness of nativism in language teaching. It is not uncommon to find that EL students are sometimes regarded as 'less intelligent' based on their lower English proficiency (Norton, 2012; Webster & Lu, 2012). This oversimplified categorization of immigrated students can be detrimental in many ways, including damaging to a student's self-concept (Norton, 2012).

Oppression on a mental level might make or force the oppressed to 'think' in the following ways that reflect internalized biases such as gender bias, racial bias, social bias and so forth: 'I can't do this, I am inferior to the rich/intelligent people in power (social bias). I, as a non-White person, am born with this unintelligent brain (racial bias). I can't master science because I am a girl (gender bias). I can't go to college, I'd better to go to a factory, as I am from a poor family and nobody in my family went to college (economic bias)'. This type of *fatalism* (Freire, 1996) or *internalized oppression* (Fanon, 2008) is at the core of self-doubt. The fatalistic mindset is imposed, forced and indoctrinated implicitly and explicitly as illustrated in the examples above, and it is reinforced through multifaceted ways in our society. In education, these fatalistic viewpoints can be reinforced through interactions between a teacher and students and between students and their peers. Research found that students even indirectly internalize an 'oppressed mindset' from the power dynamics illustrated among school administrations and field teachers (Anyon, 1980; Bernstein, 1971).

Oppression in the form of gaps or unequal access to materialistic/ tangible/superficial resources and the effects of this on one's mind is dynamically alive, subtly but closely intertwined with social injustice because it harms the students. An L2 teacher would do well to have an awareness of these notions of social justice, injustice and oppression, because 'language' is at the center of both tangible and mental resources in human rights and identity (Canagarajah, 2006).

The concept of social justice, by nature, is dynamically interrelated with the notions and considerations of race, privilege, socioeconomic status (gaps), equity, diversity, culture and identity (Coney, 2016). In teaching practices, and especially for language teaching, social justice can incorporate concepts of empowering toward, co-ownership of and questioning conceptions of socially made paradigms, biases and unequal power structures. This book uses a social justice lens as an overarching theoretical framework for exploring the lives of ELs and their perceptions of English language learning. Other frameworks such as investment (Norton-Peirce, 1995) and push, pull, fall out (Doll *et al.*, 2013) are adapted to explore the phenomenon with more dynamic viewpoints, which will be introduced in the next section.

Research Trend: Continuum and Gaps in SLA Studies

Richard-Amato (1988), an L2 teaching methodology scholar, views L2 learning as complex. He argues that L2 learning is cognitively made and affectively influenced, which is consistent with Krashen's (1982) notion of the importance of learners' affective filters. In brief, Krashen's (1982) affective filter argument focuses on the multifaceted affective domains of learning, such as anxiety, confidence, belief and feelings. People process language input cognitively and affectively. For decades, SLA researchers have tried to gain a theoretical understanding of how people really learn an L2.

From the 1960s to the 1970s, behaviorism-based English teaching methods, such as grammar translation and audio-lingual methods, were popular (Brooks, 1975; Lado, 1964; Saville-Troike, 1973). By their nature, these behaviorism-based L2 teaching methods focused on memorization and mimicking. In the 1980s, researchers put an additional focus on language input and learners' affective aspects such as anxiety. Krashen's (1982) monitor model and i + 1 hypothesis are well-known examples. Later, scholars highlighted Chomskian perspectives, such as the innatist view, which led L2 researchers and teachers to view students from more organic viewpoints (Chomsky, 1980; Hauser *et al.*, 2002).

DeKeyser (1998) and Schmidt (2001) argued that learners must pay attention to the target language features to master an L2. The term 'information processing' was introduced, emphasizing how to help students 'process' language input with in-class exercises or tasks, e.g. jigsaw activity (Anderson, 1995; DeKeyser, 1998; VanPatten, 2004). These information processing scholars argued that language learning is 'skill learning'; the process starts with declarative knowledge and through practice, it becomes procedural knowledge. For example, many scholars have studied how to teach vocabulary more efficiently through information processing (Brown & Perry, 1991; Cho & Krashen, 1994; Huckin & Coady, 1999; Jianzhong, 2003). Scholars have also studied ESL writing in terms of how to teach L2 writing more effectively (Hamp-Lyons, 1991; Harklau *et al.*, 1999; Sullivan & Pratt, 1996; Zhang, 1995). This view sees L2 learning as cognitive development.

It was critiqued by scholars who saw language learning as more of an organic human meaning-making process (following a Vygotskian sociocultural perspective), through interpersonal interactions and intrapersonal reflections (Celce-Murcia, 2008; Donato, 1994; Dunn & Lantolf, 1998; Long, 1983, 1996; Swain, 1995, 2005, 2009).

Empirical studies of the ESL profession have investigated a plethora of approaches to language learning including behavioristic, cognitive and sociocultural approaches. Although Krashen (1982) and Richard-Amato (1988) argued the importance of affective aspects in L2 learning, studies focusing on affective domains were less researched compared to other domains in the 1980s literature.

Since the 1990s, scholars such as Peirce (1995) and Cummins (1994) have pointed out the importance of affective and organic factors in L2 learning, such as identity, power relations and sociopolitical aspects inside and outside the classroom. Adult populations, marginalized by their social status (such as immigrants or refugees), may have affective aspects more susceptible to social and economic factors outside the classroom. Some L2 motivation researchers have reframed their research focus on the dynamic interrelatedness between motivation and leaner identity (Dörnyei, 2005; Giddens, 1991; Lamb, 2004; Pavlenko, 2002).

Dörnyei (2005) argued that the 'ideal' self and the 'ought-to' self can be strong motivational factors for L2 learning because mastering L2 proficiency can promote a student's ideal self. Giddens (1991) and Lamb (2004) focused more on the external environment, in which the globalization phenomenon naturally motivates students to master English as a world language. Adopting a post-structural perspective, Pavlenko (2002) challenges the traditional notion of L2 learning motivation to broaden its concepts to wider contexts by arguing that the 21st century has witnessed that more than half of the total population on Earth are already members of *multiple* ethnic, social and cultural communities. Hence, the researchers call for a paradigmatic shift in L2 motivation research. Norton-Peirce's (1995) concept of investment addressed another facet of this reconceptualization of L2 motivation and identity, because investing in L2 learning means investing in oneself. One critical assumption that Norton-Peirce (1995) offered was that the investing and self (or identity) concepts are socially constructed. A more detailed review about the theory of investment will follow.

Investment: Ideology, Identity and Capital

Expanding Norton's notions of ELs' investment (McKinney & Norton, 2008; Norton, 1997, 2012; Norton & McKinney, 2011; Norton-Peirce, 1995), Darvin and Norton (2015) developed a theoretical framework about L2 learner's investment that consists of three specific constructs: ideology, identity and capital. Inspired by Bourdieu's (1977, 1984) approaches and Blommaert's (2010) sociolinguistic approach, Darvin and Norton developed a post-structural framework to examine what comprises an individual learner's investment in systemic ways. Within such a framework, the concepts of ideology, identity and capital work together in an intertwined way, sometimes supporting and contradicting each other, in influencing one's decisions to invest in micro and macro levels of English learning.

First, *ideology* in this framework refers to a 'normative set of ideas' (Darvin & Norton, 2015: 43). The meaning of this concept in this framework is that individuals are consistently negotiating and positioning their spaces in society, communication sites and learning institutes based on the hegemony or power structure dictated by the given ideology. For example, a student might feel that their English pronunciation is not good enough to talk to people who speak English as their L1. The hegemony and ideology in this example are that they privilege native English speakers' ways of using English language as the only 'right' way or as a more 'superior' way of speaking than the students' variant forms of pronunciation. Darvin and Norton (2015) view ideology or hegemony embedded in an L2 learning context as influencing the students' decisions on investment. As ideology is a dominant way of thinking to determine inclusion and exclusion, this hegemony comprises one component of students' investment dynamics.

Second, *identity* in this framework is 'multiple, a site of struggle, and continually changing over time and space' (Darvin & Norton, 2015: 45). Influenced by ideologies based on their own ideology (based on their backgrounds) and the new ideology encountered in an English-speaking country, L2 learners' identity is by nature multiple and has the potential to shift moment by moment. At each moment, individuals either accord or refuse their power to speak. For example, a student who learns ESL might feel that their English speaking is not legitimate enough to join a learning *site* because their English accent is not legitimate enough to participate with other fluent English speakers. In this case, the student refuses their right to speak, thus learn, based on the hegemony mindset that they deserve to be excluded. On the other hand, when the person perceives that a situation is where they can speak up for their right to speak, the student accords the power to themselves and begins speaking and learning. For example, a student can ask a conversation interlocutor to slow down their speech so they can understand and communicate better. In this case, according to Darvin and Norton (2015), this student seems to centralize their identity within the site of learning (i.e. the conversation situation) by positioning their identity inside the conceptual site. Learners' imagined identity also plays a role in one's investment such as imagining becoming a successful English-speaking business owner, which can be rephrased as the perceived benefits of their investment.

Third, *capital* in this framework has three sub-constructs: economic capital, cultural capital and social capital. Darvin and Norton adapted Bourdieu's (1987) notions of these three constructs, with each standing for different characteristics of capital, all of which mean *power*:

- *Economic capital* refers to wealth, property, and income,
- *Cultural capital* refers to knowledge, educational credentials, and appreciations,
- *Social capital* refers to connections to network of power. (Darvin & Norton, 2015: 44)

What is more important about this capital notion is that the value of each is determined by ideology and one's negotiation based on the context (time and place) in which an individual encounters the capitals. The types and values of capitals are taken 'once they are perceived and recognized as legitimate' (Bourdieu, 1987: 4). Therefore, capital is fluid and dynamic, subject to the ideologies of specific groups, which is called symbolic capital (Bourdieu, 1987). Symbolic capital includes two key ideas for language teachers. First, learners enter the learning space equipped with their capital such as material resources, linguistic knowledge and social networks. Second, when learners occupy new learning spaces, they not only acquire new resources but also utilize their own capital as affordances and transform them to resources that are valuable in the context. Therefore, ESL teachers should treat the learners' linguistic and cultural capitals more as affordances than constraints.

Darvin and Norton (2015) viewed these three components toward one's investment as related to each other; they support, complement and sometimes contradict each other based on the situatedness of individual students. Figure 2.1 demonstrates Darvin and Norton's model of investment. The shared space between two concepts shows the relationship between them. For example, affordances/perceived benefits between identity and capital mean that capital can provide affordances to one's identity building efforts (e.g. enabling internet access to online learners). Perceived benefits are based on the learners' imagined identity, which in turn help the leaner to seek adequate forms of capital. Between identity and ideology, positioning refers to an individual's position negotiations between inclusion and exclusion. In an L2 learning situation, this might mean inclusion and exclusion toward L2 practice opportunities with a native speaker of the target language. The systemic patterns of control

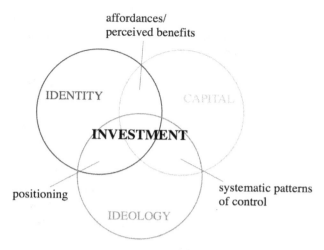

affordances/
perceived benefits

IDENTITY   CAPITAL

INVESTMENT

positioning   systematic patterns
                               of control

IDEOLOGY

Figure 2.1 Model of investment (author created diagram based on the work of Darvin and Norton [2015: 42])

between ideology and capital refer to a socially constructed environment that either supports or constrains one's access to capital. For example, economically disadvantaged students seem to encounter systematic patterns of control that prevent them from accessing internet connections, whereas affluent students can access internet resources (Darvin & Norton, 2015). 'Language as investment' provides a framework for exploring and analyzing what makes adult ELs invest or not invest in their English learning.

Push, Pull, Falling Out

Nationwide studies have been conducted concerning high school student dropout factors (Balfanz & Fox, 2011; Bureau of Labor Statistics, 2005; Cairns *et al.*, 1989; Doll *et al.*, 2013; Eckland, 1972; Englund *et al.*, 2008; Ensminger *et al.*, 1996; Griffin & Alexander, 1978; Powers & Wojtkiewicz, 2003; Rotermund, 2007). Among those, Doll *et al.*'s (2013) comparative analysis over seven nationwide quantitative studies provides a framework for the causes of high school students' dropping out, such as push, pull and falling out factors.

First, 'push' refers to any pressure from inside the school that leads students to drop out, such as negative test results, attendance issues and discipline policies (Jordan *et al.*, 1994). 'Pull' refers to distracting components inside a student that constrain the student from completing school, such as 'financial worries, out-of-school employment, family needs, and even family changes' (Doll *et al.*, 2013: 2). Lastly, Watt and Roessingh (1994) argued about the third factor of 'falling out' that refers to a situation where a student dislikes school and gains no academic interest due to the circumstances around that student. The key distinctions among push, pull and falling out lie in agency; with push, the school is the agent, whereas for pull a student is the agent. However, falling out's agent is neither the school nor a student; the agent is 'circumstances that exist that neither the school nor the student can remediate, and as a result, the connection students have with school gradually diminishes' (Doll *et al.*, 2013: 2).

Falling out is not an active decision, rather an involuntarily forced choice of leaving school. Watt and Roessingh (1994, 2001) found that falling out decisions are forced by many situational reasons such as educational budget cuts, the necessity of financially supporting family by part-time jobs, fatigue and lack of sleep due to work, and fear of being punished for unfinished homework derived from their socially structured tiring life. Among push, pull and falling out factors, Doll *et al.* (2013) found that pulling was the most dominant cause, followed by push and falling out. This book adopted this framework to explore dropout factors for the adult ELs who enrolled in an evening English literacy class.

Situatedness of Immigrant Adult Learners of English Literacy

Because one's identity and investment are influenced by one's situatedness (Lave & Wenger, 1991), and considering that the fundamental inquiry of this book is *What makes adult ELs either persist or drop out?*, I would emphasize the importance of the situatedness of adult ELs to explore the target phenomenon more plausibly. The themes found through previous research of adult learners' learning motivation seem to converge into four themes: job, family, self-actualization and being a community member in a new society (Vafai, 2016; Valentine, 1990; Wang, 2006). However, the population for each study has shown different priority patterns. Valentine (1990) shows that personal development is the number one desire for ELs, whereas Wang (2006) and Vafai (2016) show that job needs were preeminent. The need of many ELs for academic purposes is to pass a standardized test, such as the test of English as a foreign language (TOEFL) or the International English Language Testing System (IELTS), in order to pursue higher education in English-speaking countries (Hsieh, 2017). On the contrary, immigrant adult ELs for community purposes have different needs based on the four aforementioned themes for their functional and transitional desires (Auerbach, 1993). Understanding the different 'situatedness' between ELs for academic and community purposes is important because that situatedness foregrounds different goals and characteristics of adult ELs (Gee, 2012, 2014; Lave & Wenger, 1991). Menard-Warwick (2005) expanded the adult ELs' situation by considering the larger sociopolitical issues surrounding students, closely related to governmental policies toward immigrants in the US. For example, the 2016 US presidential candidate Donald

Trump's pledge to expel undocumented immigrants (Wang, 2016) would have directly affected the immigrated adult students. Thus, the situatedness of students must be explored with multiple lenses to shed light on adult ELs' investment factors for learning English.

Holistic and Ecological Nature of SLA

For decades, SLA scholars have studied how to teach content knowledge more effectively such as how to teach phonics, speech skills, writing skills and so on (Larsen-Freeman, 1997; Lightbown & Spada, 2013; Swain, 2005). However, affective aspects in L2 learning are as important as how to teach content knowledge, which seems to call scholars and teachers' attention to a more ecological and comprehensive approach to SLA, ranging from sociopolitical concerns, psychological aspects, cultural considerations, learner identity, investment and the social responsibility of English teaching. SLA scholars have devised an ecological approach to SLA by integrating the diverse and dynamic nature of L2 learning called the transdisciplinary framework (Costa & Norton, 2017; Douglas Fir Group, 2016). Composed of renowned SLA scholars such as Merrill Swain, Bonny Norton and Diane Larsen-Freeman, the Douglas Fir Group has developed the multifaceted nature of language learning and teaching in 2016 depicted in Figure 2.2. In this framework, the nature of L2 learning is multifaceted, multilayered and consistently evolving over time, ranging from the macro level of ideological structures (belief systems, cultural values), the meso level of sociocultural institutions and communities (social identities, families, place of work) and the micro

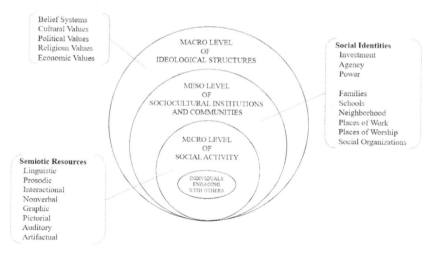

Figure 2.2 The multifaceted nature of language learning and teaching (author created diagram based on the work of the Douglas Fir Group [2016: 25])

level of social activities (individual engaging with semiotic resources). The aforementioned investment framework is located in the meso-level layer of social identities. It is imperative that ESL teachers and stakeholders grapple with the nature of the multilayeredness of L2 learning.

This book has used three theoretical frameworks: investment (Darvin & Norton, 2015), push/pull/fall out (Doll *et al.*, 2013) and a holistic approach to language learning (Douglas Fir Group, 2016). Among these, the main framework is investment, that is related to learner's identity; thus, it also relates to social justice to some extent. Push/pull/fall out is related to social justice, because the dropout factor constructs are socially constructed. Finally, the holistic approach to language learning is related to the situatedness of learners and investment, because it shows the interwoven and multifaceted nature of one's language learning.

3 Adult English Literacy Learners in America and Research Context

Adult English Literacy Learners: Who Are They?

In 2019, 17.4% of the US workforce (28.4 million) were immigrants (US Department of Labor, 2020). The number of foreign-born workers increased from 23 million in 2006 to 28.4 million in 2019. Of the 28.4 million foreign-born workers in the US, almost half were Latinx and 30% were Asian. One of the most difficult barriers for the immigrated workforce is language (Valentine, 1990). According to the Office of Career, Technical, and Adult Education (2020), adult English learners (ELs) enrolled in adult English literacy classes numbered 1.1 million in 2019–2020, which means that over 20 million ELs were not enrolled. Tucker (2006) reported that adult EL classes in the US have long waiting lists of up to three years. Among the students enrolled nationwide, Latinx learners accounted for 44%. In Oklahoma, Latinx ELs accounted for 35% of adult language learners (Office of Career, Technical, and Adult Education, 2019). Many jobs available to ELs may entail risk of physical accident, and their lack of English proficiency may keep them revolving around the margins of the job market (Hopkins, 2002; Navarez, 2015). Studies have shown that adult foreign-born workers' employability is related to English proficiency (Hyman, 2002; Mathews-Aydinli, 2008). In 2021, adult education grants totaled $688 million, only 0.7% of the US education budget ($95,545 million) (US Department of Education, 2021).

Term Matters: ESL, EFL, ELL and EL

Several different terms refer to learners of English as an additional language other than their first language (L1) based on learning contexts. One relatively simple clarification between English as a second language (ESL) and English as a foreign language (EFL) is whether a learner lives in the target language-speaking country or in a country that does not speak the target language (Nayar, 1997). The former is called 'second language' and the latter is called 'foreign language'. For example, if a student from Mexico learns English and lives in the US simultaneously, the setting is called ESL. In the teaching English to speakers of other languages (TESOL) field, ESL is widely used to refer to academic ELs who learn English to pursue their higher education in an English-speaking country (Nayar, 1997). On the contrary, when a Mexican student living in Mexico learns English at a school in Mexico, this situation is called EFL.

Another term, English language learning (ELL), seems to be categorized under the concept of ESL, with the individual living in a country where a second language is used. In the US, ELL refers to K-12 students whose L1 is a language other than English, and who have less proficiency in English. However, one issue with using the term ELL is that the term has a somewhat negative connotation that any student labeled as ELL is 'positioned in a category outside the category of mainstream language learners in the classroom' (English, 2009, cited in Lee & Lu, 2012). A student categorized as ELL may give the impression that the student is at the margins of society (Hastings & Jacob, 2016). Language is power and can be used as a means of keeping people at the margins of society (Freire, 1996).

This critique seems to lead to a discussion of the necessity for an alternative term for ELL. The new term, English learners, was introduced by the Every Student Succeeds Act (ESSA) signed by the US Department of Education in December 2015 (Alicandri, 2016). Since the ESSA, many US states have begun to use the term (Oklahoma State Department of Education, 2017). However, several government agencies and public schools still use the term ELL (National Center for Education Statistics, n.d.; Oklahoma State Department of Education, 2015).

For adult immigrated populations who learn English in the US for non-academic purposes, EL seems appropriate and has 'less baggage' than other terms. This study uses 'English learner' to refer to Spanish-speaking adult learners who learn English at a literacy center through evening classes.

Adult English Literacy Class Characteristics

The adult ELs' learning environment seems hard to characterize with precision. Unlike in K-12 schools, adult EL courses have a wider age range, from 16 to 90+, and students with a variety of educational backgrounds ranging from no education to PhDs (Comings, 2007; Mathews-Aydinli, 2008). The classroom venues for adult ELs tend to be diverse – a public library meeting room, a cafeteria or a classroom in a local church (Han, 2009; Menard-Warwick, 2005; Peirce et al., 1993; Schalge & Soga, 2008). The adult students' desire to invest is generally high, regardless of their backgrounds or language proficiency because adult ELs must go to class in their 'free' time (Bernat, 2004; Derwing, 2003; Hyman, 2002; Valentine, 1990). Despite their high willingness in English learning investment, poor learning outcomes are recurring problems (Bernat, 2004; Office of Career, Technical, and Adult Education, 2019). The National Assessment of Adult Literacy (NAAL) reported that in recent years, Latinx adults' English prose levels (written or spoken language) have fallen dramatically (from 234 to 216, which is almost Below Basic) (National Assessment of Adult Literacy, 2005). The Office of Career, Technical, and Adult Education (2019) reports that adult English literacy learners' skill gain rate was 46% in 2013–2016, but it decreased to about 36% in 2019. Another consideration for the adult EL context is the teachers' unique characteristics. Most adult EL teachers are either volunteers or part-timers; job security is relatively low and appropriately trained teachers are rare (Mathews-Aydinli, 2008).

Center for English Literacy (CEL) in This Study

The CEL is a non-profit English teaching institute located in an urban city in the Southwestern US. The CEL's primary funding sources are from various grants, donations and fundraising events. The CEL was founded in the 1980s to address adult illiteracy by helping adults improve their basic literacy and math skills. The head office is located in the city's downtown, and teachers work day and night at satellite locations to teach adult ELs. In 2017, when I taught at the CEL, 13 teachers worked as part-time teachers and 17 satellite classrooms were operating across the city. Classes usually had an enrollment of 5–10 students, mostly refugees and immigrants. Student numbers fluctuated for many reasons, including family issues and time conflicts. I taught English to refugee and immigrant groups from Mexico, Myanmar, Vietnam, Panama and Chile at the CEL for four years. The teaching venues included a break room in a metal valve manufacturing factory, a library meeting room in an elementary school and a room in a local church.

Participant Characteristics and Methods

The participants in this study were six adult Latinx ELs, who enrolled in and studied at a non-profit community literacy institute in a city in the Southwestern US. Most of the students had day jobs in fields such as construction, housekeeping and manufacturing. Their ages ranged from 20 to 50. They had resided in the US from less than 5 years to more than 20 years. All the participants were from Mexico and their L1 was Spanish. I taught English to these students in the fall of 2016. The two-hour class met twice a week (Mondays and Wednesdays). The class used the Basic English Skill Test (BEST) Literacy developed by the Center for Applied Linguistics as a pre- and post-test to evaluate students' progress. However, the BEST Literacy that my class used has only reading and writing components to assess – no speaking or listening. Although the test developer launched Best Plus 2.0 that includes oral assessment in 2016 (Center for Applied Linguistics, 2021), the CEL used the previous BEST only in 2017.

To explore untold adult ELs' stories: (1) I interviewed the six participants about what makes them invest in English classes and what makes them drop out; (2) I observed and took photographs of their lives at home, at work and in classes; and (3) I kept field notes and memos for my reflection and interpretation of the phenomenon. I used semi-structured interviews and each participant's interview was conducted for one to one and a half hours. The interview questions consisted of open-ended questions to listen to the participants' voices. Example questions include: In your life, what makes you feel that you want to (or don't want to) learn English more? (probing question); and Okay, you said _____ made you think that you want to (or don't want to) learn English more. What specific aspects made you feel that way? Can you give me any examples?

I collected the data and interacted with the participants for 19 months, from May 2016 to November 2017. Note that in the interview data some students said that they wanted to learn English and work with me (teacher John) again, and I have represented their true words but I don't want it to be mistaken for self-praise. Also, throughout this book, the participants' original narratives with grammar or vocabulary mistakes are used in order to maintain authenticity.

Adult EL Stories through My Eyes: Subjectivity Statement

As is the nature of a qualitative study (Creswell, 2012), it is essential for me to clarify my subjectivity. Because I was a researcher outside of the study population group, the data collected were interpreted through my eyes. As a qualitative researcher, I clarify my subjectivity for bracketing my unforeseen bias when collecting, analyzing and interpreting the data and phenomenon. I uphold the constructivism that values the multiple realities based on individuals (Guba & Lincoln, 1994). I agree that the data interpretation is constructed by the interactions between the participants and myself as a researcher, and I acknowledge that my interpretation is a plausible facet of the multiple realities (Shank, 2002). Therefore, I am open to other interpretations respecting the constructivism.

I was born and raised in South Korea. My maternal grandparents lived in the northern region of the Korean Peninsula before the Korean War broke out in 1950. To avoid the warzone, they moved to South Korea, where my mother was born. When I was young, I thought of my mother's family as poor, but they 'became' poor because of the war. Before the war, they had a house, money and land. The government said that the war would end in a few months, but many people living in the north, including my mother's siblings, moved to the south to avoid the conflict. Once they had moved to South Korea, it was not possible to return to the north and it has remained impossible for the past 70 years.

On the contrary, originating in the south, my father's family was influential and possessed land and money. To make a long story short, it seems that the Korean War made my mother's family poor and my father's family rich.

I have always liked language, whether Korean, Chinese or English. I served in the Korean Air Force as a weather forecaster for nine years, and then worked at a semiconductor company for four years. These jobs were okay, but not creative; thus, I asked myself what I wanted to do for the rest of my life. The answer was to become a language educator, so I came to the US to earn my master's and doctorate degrees in second language teaching. After receiving my master's in teaching English to speakers of other languages (MA TESOL), I taught at academic ESL centers, where many international students go to study English prior to entering US colleges. At the same time, I worked at a non-profit literacy center that sent ESL teachers to high-need areas. For one year, I taught refugees from Myanmar, Mexico and Panama in a factory's cafeteria. I also taught adult Latinx students at a local elementary school and church. At a hotel, I taught a group of housekeeping staff who had moved to the US from Latin America.

Over the course of about six years, these language teaching experiences were creative and rewarding as an educator. However, when it was time to ponder my doctorate dissertation research topic, I decided to work with immigrants, not college prep students. I asked myself why I wanted to work with them, and it seems that, because I had family members marginalized by the post-Korean War sociocultural structure in East Asia, I was interested in working with adult ELs who are members of marginalized populations in the US. The ELs whom I worked with were called 'illegals' and 'border rats' (Macedo, 2000), and were 'subject to deportation'. With the Trump administration's radical immigration policy during January 2017–January 2021 (Wang, 2016), I began to feel my students' sense of security was shaken, just as my mother's family status in South Korea in the 1950s was shaken.

As an ESL teacher, I went by an English nickname 'John'. Because I am a non-native speaker of English, I was somewhat worried about my class, which made me prepare hard and approach my teaching in a deliberate way. As mentioned in the introduction, I had two substitute teachers take over when I was absent for two months due to health reasons; I didn't worry at all because my substitutes were native speakers of English. However, when I returned, my students said that they learned nothing from the subs. If I were my students, I would be more likely to welcome native speaker teachers than non-native speaker teachers. However, that was not the case. After listening to their narratives, I realized that such student stories often go unheard, especially by ESL stakeholders. This qualitative study describes the untold, socioculturally situated and ongoing journey of immigrants to learn English in America.

The Purpose of This Book

This book focuses on students' identity-level meaning making as a subjective and active participant in second language learning. First, this book explores adult ESL students' needs for learning English. Second, it investigates diverse possible factors that might impact adult students' desire for learning English. Third, it explores the untold stories of English learning journeys and decision-making rationales. In other words, it reveals what learning English means to ELs, and what made them persist or drop out of English class. The questions that this book pursues answer to are

- Who are adult ELs at the CEL?
- Why do adult ELs at the CEL invest in learning English?
- What makes adult ELs at the CEL decide to stay or drop out?

The untold stories and voices of adult immigrant ELs in the US will be heard in Chapter 4.

4 The Six Persistent Learners

Irma's Story

I need English to protect my kids. My two daughters, 9 and 11 year old, translated in an emergency room 18 years ago when my ex-husband died due to cancer…it was so hard, so sad. I couldn't speak any English, couldn't protect my kids. I wanted to tell the doctors, 'talk to me, don't touch my kids', but I couldn't. I always want to learn English, but I dropped my English class, because the teacher didn't care for us, never prepared for the class. We did the same thing for three days. It was waste of time.

Irma (pseudonym) is from Mexico. She is 51 years old and has lived in the US for 27 years. She was born in Mexico and came to the US with her husband to work. Irma's two daughters, Samantha and Eli (pseudonyms), were born in Texas. Irma has done many different physical jobs, including hand-picking grapes and berries, making medical equipment and bags in a factory, nursing elderly people and making cardboard. Irma is proud of herself for working full-time in the US, and prefers factory work to other jobs, saying, 'I like factory working more than other jobs like housekeeping and restaurant. I worked at a factory for 16 years. It is easy and comfortable for me'. She had difficult times at work due to her lack of English proficiency. 'No English, heavy work', Irma said. When she started her first factory job at the medical equipment factory, her boss asked her to carry a heavy box. To Irma, the box was way too heavy to carry. She wanted to say that she couldn't do it, but she didn't know how to say it, so she just mumbled. Her boss pushed her to do it anyway. Irma ended up carrying the box, hurting her back. Avoiding work exploitation is one reason for Irma to learn English.

Recently, Irma is very proud of her English at work, because she is a translator between her boss and her colleagues. Irma's boss looks for Irma to communicate work orders with other Mexican workers. 'I am so happy when my boss called me, I translate, and we both understand', Irma said. Her two colleagues, Marcella and Ibby (pseudonyms), asked

Irma about her command of English. 'Irma, English very good! Where did you learn?' 'I have my good teacher John'. Irma wanted to bring her two colleagues to my class one day.

Irma's top reason to learn English is to protect her children. Eighteen years ago, her ex-husband was sent to an emergency room. Irma spoke zero English, so her two daughters, 9 and 11 years old, translated what was going on. Later that night, they translated that their father had died. 'It was so hard, so sad, John. I wanted to protect my kids, but I couldn't, because I don't know any English', Irma said. Since that night, Irma's motivation to learn English has never gone away. She took and completed three English as a second language (ESL) classes held at a community college and an elementary school. She recalls that, 'I finished the schools, but I don't remember anything'.

She came to my class in August 2016. Irma was an active student and never missed any classes. She always did her homework and contributed to group discussions. Irma was a lead student for the self-presentation activity in which students drew a picture of their portrait and wrote explanations of it (Figure 4.1). Her English proficiency was higher than her other classmates, probably because she has lived in the US for 27 years. Irma translated my class content to classmates, enjoyed the homework I gave by approaching it meaningfully and projecting her life and stories into it. For example, when we studied the phrase 'even though', the sentences Irma wrote for her homework were 'Even though I became a widow, I bought a house' and 'Even though I turned 51 yesterday, I feel like 25'. It was her life story. We reflected on her first sentence for her perseverance to live independently without her husband. And for the second sentence, we all happily laughed. I was surprised how witty and deep Irma's approach was to English class (Figure 4.2).

Although Irma had a strong desire to learn English, she dropped out when the new substitute came in during my sick leave in November 2016. Irma thought the substitute didn't care about the students at all because he didn't prepare for the class and instead just said, 'What do you want to learn today?'. Irma had the impression that the teacher just came in to sit with them. Irma recalled that one day the substitute even went back home during the class time because he had forgotten his journal. The teacher talked about movies, which made Irma more frustrated, because Irma said, 'What movies? I have never seen any movies in this country'. The movie topic could be a good topic for pre-collegiate students who study English for their higher education, but not for these adult learners. 'Teacher Derek (the first substitute teacher) didn't prepare, just talked about movies, He taught the same thing – ABC alphabets for three days. Waste of time, so I quit', Irma said. Irma dropped out after three months.

In summer 2017, I interviewed Irma and visited her church. One day, Irma and Domingo came to me to talk about their new approach to English learning. 'John, can you teach us at any time you are available? We

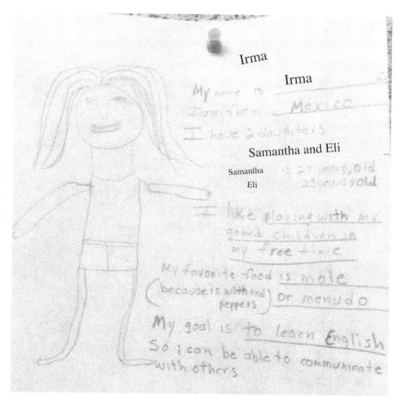

Figure 4.1 Irma's self-portrait she drew for the self-presentation activity. Irma was a lead and model student for this activity for peers (*pseudonyms are used for Irma and her children)

don't want other teachers, we want you to teach us'. We started a kind of 'Sunday English school' at their church. Irma brought her two colleagues, Marcella and Ibby, to the Sunday school. We had total of five students for the Sunday school: Irma, Domingo, Marcella, Ibby and Chris (Chris is the sixth participant of this study). From August to October 2017, we met every Sunday from 3pm to 5pm, to study English. Reflecting on the students' needs and wants, we practiced sentences, phrases, how to pronounce English sounds by using group work, presentations and homework assignment sharing. All the students seemed happy to come, and Marcella accounted that 'I have never seen Ibby smiling and laughing like this. She enjoys this class. We work together for 10 years, it's my first time to see her happy'. Like Irma's 'even though' examples, it seemed that Ibby took the class not only to learn English, but also to reflect on her life and grow through it. When the weather grew cold in November 2017 and the Thanksgiving break came, we momentarily stopped our Sunday school.

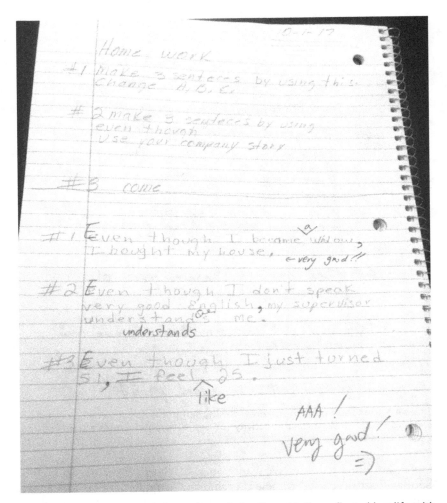

Figure 4.2 Irma's homework for a phrase 'even though'. She reflected her life with a deep and witty approach

Irma is a documented immigrant. Irma and Samantha travelled back and forth to Mexico over the Thanksgiving break to visit Irma's mother living in Mexico.

Mag's Story

I am a hard worker. My boss likes me because I make 50 drawers during my shift, while my night shift people make 40. I wanted to improve my English for a promotion opportunity, but dropped out because I felt it is a waste of time.

Mag (pseudonym) is from Chihuahua, Mexico. She is 27 years old and a mother of two daughters and one son. Mag crossed the border with her two daughters four years ago, and her son was born in the US with her new husband whom she met in Oklahoma. Her current husband, Mario (pseudonym) is 43 years old and has lived in the US for 17 years. Mag is proud of her hard work in a furniture manufacturing company. Her husband called Mag 'a nail gunner' because Mag uses a nail gun to assemble wood drawers.

She came to the Center for English Literacy's (CEL) English class in September 2016, because her boss offered her a better position – working inside. However, this offer was conditional upon having better English proficiency. Mag's English proficiency was basic, but good enough to comprehend some everyday English. She was an active learner, always smiling and working well with her classmates although she looked tired. During break time, she smoked outside with a few classmates. Mag's English proficiency was the lowest among the 20 students in my class, but her classmates helped her in a supportive manner. Figure 4.3 shows Mag's illustration of herself on self-presentation day. On returning to class after my winter off owing to a health issue, Mag was one of three other students who showed up for the new class. When I interviewed her, she said she had dropped out in March 2017, when another teacher, Amy (pseudonym), took over. Mag said, 'I dropped out because the class was waste of time. I learn nothing. The teacher didn't care about us'.

In return for interviewing her, she invited me to her house in Oklahoma City. Her husband owns the house and they rent a room to a single Mexican man. As Mag's English proficiency is basic, her husband helped with the interview as a translator. Mario's English proficiency is higher than Mag's, and he seemed to have no problem conducting day-to-day interactions in English. Sometimes, Mag directly answered interview questions. During the interview, Mag's husband unexpectedly dominated the conversation. Mario graduated high school in Mexico and came to the US to financially support his mother 17 years ago. He traveled across many states to build houses and buildings, worked as a custom painter for houses and built the mansion of the magnate who owned a big furniture company in Oklahoma City. Mario constantly hugged his and Mag's son during the interview, but never called nor looked at the daughters. Their kitchen was under construction. Mario said they were remodeling the kitchen by using the drawers that Mag's company sells, and lumber and wood doors that Mario's current workplace uses.

Mario supports Mag's English learning, and at the same time, somewhat oppresses Mag to not to actively learn English. For example, Mag said that she could accommodate her schedule to come to the English language class on Monday and Wednesday nights provided the teacher was good. However, Mario intervened by saying, 'Mag needs to think again, because we go to a Bible study every Wednesday'. They are Catholic, and the Bible study is held in Spanish. In an aside, Mag said to me that

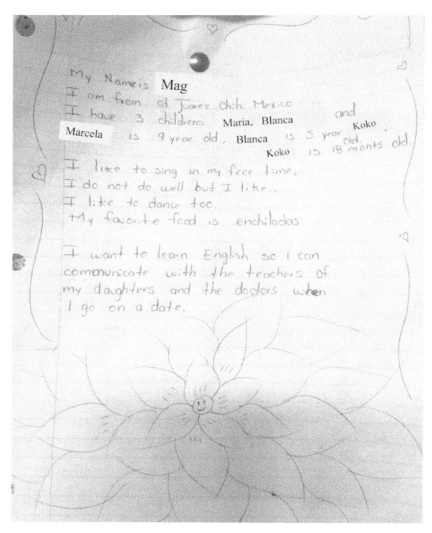

Figure 4.3 Mag's self-portrait that she drew on presentation day using English (*pseudonyms are used for Mag and her children)

she could accommodate her Wednesday night schedule. Also, a translator who helped me to transcribe the Spanish conversations between Mag and Mario in the interview pointed out that there is probably a gender-based tension between Mario and Mag, because the translator picked up several expressions in Mario's Spanish conversations to Mag, such as 'digale' (meaning 'go, tell!') and 'dile!' (meaning 'tell him!'). The translator, from Mexico, pointed out that Mario may have been showing machismo to indicate he was the head of the household.

Mag is a documented immigrant with a working visa. She crossed the border for her daughters' futures, because Mag said it is hard to live in Mexico. Mario and Mag both argued that everything is unfair in Mexico. If you have no money, you cannot proceed with any education regardless of your intelligence. Monetary compensation is not fair either; you cannot buy a car or a house although you work hard. They feel that the US is fairer and gives them more opportunities. For example, McDonald's was mentioned more than 10 times during the interview. Mario said that going to a McDonald's in Mexico is a luxurious activity only for rich people, whereas in the US, anyone can go. In the US, they have their own house and cars, and can afford to go to a McDonald's anytime.

Mario pushed her to say, 'I am a hard worker'. When Mag repeated the words, she seemed deflated. She seemed nervous and unmotivated to say words prompted by Mario. However, her desire to learn sometimes emerged naturally. When we said good-bye and walked to the door of their house, Mag stopped me at a wall displaying her family photos and proudly talked to me in English, introducing her family both in the US and in Mexico. When discussing her family photos, Mag seemed poised and happy. 'John, this is my family in Mexico, my mom, my cousins. This is my old daughter…'. The sentence structure was complete and there was no fear of mistakes or wrong utterances. She asked me, 'John when are you coming back to teach? When is your class starting again? I want to come again'. Although she lost her promotion opportunity to a colleague with better English proficiency, Mag's motivation to learn English still seemed high.

Domingo's Story

I came to CEL to learn English to help my kids, and for more opportunities in my job. But I dropped out because I heard that the teacher said 'quiet!' to my Spanish conversation and 'stupid!' to my classmate. How can you come to class when a person calls you stupid?

Domingo (pseudonym), 33 years old, is from Mexico City and has lived in the US for 17 years. Married to Samantha (pseudonym), Domingo has three sons. After he graduated from middle school, Domingo came to the US to support his family. He recalled what his father said when Domingo was about to cross the border: 'Domingo, listen son. Make your decision now between studying and supporting your family'. 'I'll support my family', he said. Like Mario, Domingo travelled to different states to work in construction fields, including Arkansas, Georgia, Texas and California. He came back to Oklahoma after his first year-long work 'trip'. Based on his initial plan, he intended to return to Mexico, but his friend recommended that he stay in the US, because the US has more opportunities and there is good money to be made from working. Domingo followed his friend's recommendation and worked for a petroleum company, where he operated an oil valve and was paid $10 per hour. To him, it was good money and an easy job, and he decided to stay. Currently, Domingo works for a construction company as a laborer. He works with two Mexican colleagues to build houses, including roofing, plumbing and interior works, under an American boss.

Before marriage, Domingo lived with a Mexican man with the same name, Domingo. In fact, at one time Samantha was the other Domingo's girlfriend. But her husband-to-be Domingo answered the phone once, and that was how they first met. The other Domingo was deported to Mexico. After marrying, Samantha and Domingo had three sons, who were 10, 7 and 5 years old in 2017 when I met them in person. I have visited their house and church congregations more than 15 times, and they visited me at my school in fall 2017.

Domingo lived in a trailer in Oklahoma City. I had no idea about living in a trailer. The trailer 'village' was located right next to a railroad. Every two hours, you could hear how fast and loud a train can run. They didn't pay rent, but paid taxes, about $200 per year. The light-blue trailer building was quite old. Domingo had built a nice deck in front of the house and there was a small front yard where Domingo repaired his car under a tree. Domingo and I used to repair my car together. I was often amazed by his passion, concentration and creativity.

We worked on my car three times in his front yard. He used and created new tools based on what he had in his toolbox. Usually, people use a car jack pump, jack-stands made of steel and neat sets of tools that include things like a shiny brake bar. However, Domingo used piles of 2 × 4 lumber as a 'jack-stand' and a long flat plier as a jack-up pump arm because the pump was missing a bar. Previously, I had seen many people throw away a jack-up pump after losing the pumping arm, but Domingo used the plier as a new arm (Figure 4.4). The first task we did together was to replace a front CV-axle of my car. A local car mechanic wanted about $300 to do the job, but Domingo said, 'I can do it, don't waste your time and money'. Again, I was not 100% sure about his skills, but recalling the incident when he helped get my car fixed in the middle of the night, I decided to let him give it a try. More importantly, Domingo's eyes were shining when he said 'John, I can do it'.

Staying dirty was a catchphrase for car mechanics. Domingo and I were covered with dirt and oil, but successfully replaced the old CV-axle with a new one. We paid about $70 for the part. During the task, there were many frustrating moments. Some bolts and nuts were extremely tight, so we could not get them out. When we tried to take the old CV-axle out, it refused. Each moment of struggle seemed like an ordeal. Honestly, at several points, I felt like we should stop and tow my car to a professional mechanic shop. However, Domingo was very calm, relaxed and even hummed songs. Whenever we had problems, he hummed songs,

Figure 4.4 The broken jack and piles of lumber used as jack-stands

implicitly saying that 'it is not a big deal, we can do this'. I was impressed with his strong problem-solving skills, his physical capabilities and his resilience. Since that day, my car has worked well. I asked him how he knew all of the repairing logistics. He said, 'I tried lots of times. I made many mistakes, and I learn from them. For example, to get the CV-axle out, it took me three hours the other day. I asked my friend, and he came to me and used a big flat driver, it just came out. I used hammer and other pliers. I also read books and YouTube videos to learn'. Through his real-life success stories in this car-repairing saga I saw a strong potential for learning and mastering English.

Domingo came to my class in August 2016. His number one reason to learn English was that he wanted to help his children read English books. He wanted to be an active part of his children's education, life and hopes. Domingo pointed out that he didn't feel good whenever his children came to him asking about an English textbook they studied at school. All he could say was, 'I don't know, go to your mom'. Domingo mentioned that his job needs were also a reason to learn English, but helping his children was more important to him than his job. His children speak Spanish to him, but use English with their mother. Samantha was born in the US.

I visited his church for Spanish congregations on Sundays from June to September 2017. I played drums for their worship time and taught Domingo how to play drums. Domingo was a fast learner. I drew musical notes for drumbeats, and he understood pretty much everything and practiced actively, even when I was not with him. Domingo's youngest son was also interested in playing drums, so we bought two new pairs of drumsticks for Domingo and his son. On one occasion, Domingo came to me and translated into English what his Spanish pastor had said in the sermon. It was very impressive that Domingo was not nervous, but instead was calm and motivated to translate the narrative. The sermon was a metaphor on seeing the world like the fish tank shown in the movie *Finding Nemo* (2003). When the oxygen-providing machine stopped, the fish tank became dirty. The pastor's point was that Christianity is like the oxygen machine. This impromptu translation was never planned, nor requested. Domingo's urgent motivation to help me, as a non-Spanish speaker, to understand the situation in the moment seemed to motivate and empower him. I learned that Domingo became a Christian, a Protestant, six years ago. Samantha was a Christian from birth, but that was not the case for Domingo. He said he was bad because he drank every day after work. One day, he went to an emergency room, and the doctor said he had only two months to live due to a bad liver. All his family prayed for him to survive, and their prayers were answered. Since that experience, Domingo said he stopped drinking and listens to the Bible to keep his spirit 'happy and right'.

Domingo was a passionate student in my class, always doing his homework. He was the only student who did the homework assignment in which I asked students to email a message to me. I wanted to integrate e-literacy skills into the curriculum. Domingo was never absent, and opened and closed the class door every night. When I came back from my two-month leave, he was one of the students remaining. He had stayed with the class through two other instructors. However, an incident occurred that made Domingo decide to drop out. He was having a conversation with one of his classmates in Spanish when teacher Amy (the second substitute teacher) called one of his classmates 'stupid'. He said, 'How can you come to a person saying stupid to you?'.

Domingo is an undocumented immigrant who has lived in the US for 17 years. His wife and family worried about him and wanted him to complete the immigration paperwork. For some reason, he just kept saying with a smile, 'I'll do it later. I like Mexican citizenship. I don't know any reason to do the paperwork'. According to Samantha, however, Domingo's status is vulnerable to deportation. Samantha thinks Domingo may worry about any potential deportation reasons that arise when he completes the paperwork.

During the time of the study, Domingo worked with an American boss, a contractor. Domingo and his crew were subcontractors or laborers. Domingo said that his boss was paid more than he was, though the boss sits all day in his truck and does nothing while Domingo and his crew sweat outside. Domingo's one dream is to establish his own building business and to own his own construction firm. This is another reason that he wanted to improve his English.

Eva's Story

I came to the US because my husband recommended, but I said 'no' first. Upon his second suggestion after five years, we came together with my daughter. I wanted to go back to Mexico. My family lives there. But, my husband and daughter want to stay, so I stay. I wanted to learn English to communicate with people, and for everything, for my work, daughter and life; everything is English here. I always want to learn English, but I dropped because the class is no more interesting. The teacher didn't care for us. It is waste of time. I quit.

Eva (pseudonym) is 42 years old and has lived in the US for 10 years. She came to the US with her husband and daughter. When her husband asked Eva to go to the US 15 years ago, Eva said no. Upon her husband's second suggestion five years later, they came together but planned to stay only one or two years and then go back. Eva's mother and sisters are living in Mexico, so Eva always wanted to go back to Mexico. Her daughter wanted to stay in the US for a better education and more opportunities, so Eva decided to stay. Eva's husband works in construction. They bought a house in Oklahoma. Her daughter was a senior high school student when Eva started her English class in 2016. Her daughter was a college student majoring in accounting when I interviewed Eva in 2017. In spring 2017, Eva was busy preparing and celebrating her daughter's 15th birthday – quinceañera in Spanish. Quinceañera is a big event not only for the person who is turning 15 years old, but also for the whole family and the community. Eva's mother and sisters in Mexico visited Oklahoma to celebrate quinceañera together in April 2017 (Figure 4.5).

Eva works in an American restaurant in Oklahoma City. This is her tenth year working in the restaurant as food preparation staff. Eva arrives at the restaurant at 5am every morning and prepares food by cutting vegetables (Figure 4.6). She works in a kitchen with an Indian colleague. Out of eight colleagues, only Eva and one other are Spanish speakers. The others are White English speakers. Eva's colleagues sometimes push her to speak English, but Eva says, 'No, you learn Spanish'. Eva said she wanted to speak English very well, but it is sometimes hard and forcing her to speak English made her feel anxious. However, she wanted to learn English for many other reasons such as her daughter's schoolwork, grocery shopping and doctor's appointments.

Eva came to my class in August 2016. Her number one reason to learn English was that she wanted to communicate with others. She wanted to talk to people at work, her daughter's teachers and people in stores. Eva dreamed of listening and speaking good enough English to communicate freely with other people. One day, a customer asked, 'How are you?'. Eva knew that it would've been a good chance to talk and practice English with the person, so she wanted to say something like, 'I'm good, what about you?'. But she couldn't open her mouth and ended up saying, 'I

Figure 4.5 Eva's daughter explaining her quinceañera photos. Quinceañera was a major event for the community

Figure 4.6 Eva's restaurant kitchen. For 10 years, Eva has come here every day at 5am to prepare food

busy, I go'. Another example is when her chef colleagues asked her what she wanted to eat for lunch, she couldn't say anything but omelet. This desire to communicate with other people, understand others and make others understand her motivated Eva to come to adult English class.

Eva was a good student in my class: quiet but motivated. She brought her friend Elsa (the fifth participant of this book) to class. Eva and Elsa actively studied together by making presentation slides, sharing stories and doing homework (Figure 4.7). When I returned from sick leave, Eva remained with the other three students. Eva said, 'I knew you are coming back, so wait for you'. However, Eva had dropped out of the class in March 2017 when taught by teacher Amy, seven months after she started my class. She said she dropped out because the class that the other teacher taught was no longer interesting and the teacher didn't prepare lessons – they played games for three days, and eventually she learned nothing from it. Feeling that it was a waste of time, Eva dropped out.

Figure 4.7 Eva's presentation drawing on self-presentation day using English (*pseudonym is used for Eva)

For Eva, checking homework meant a lot. She said that teacher John checked her homework every class, but teacher Amy didn't usually give homework. Amy gave homework a few times, but she forgot the homework the next time. 'Amy didn't check the homework. She didn't care. I did my homework, but the teacher forgot the homework. She no care', Eva said. Eva has a strong desire to learn English. During the interview, she asked me 'how to say this in English?' many times. Also, she said, 'John, when are you coming back? I want to go back to your class'.

Eva and Elsa had been friends for 10 years. They met at an elementary school because their daughters attended the same school. Elsa ended up working weekends at Eva's restaurant as a waitress. They work, share life stories and study English together. Eva is a documented immigrant.

Elsa's Story

I want to learn English to talk to other people like my colleagues at work. Especially, I want to talk to White guys in my dance club. Everyone is White, I need to speak English. I don't like when White people hate me because I don't speak English and I look different. I didn't choose my skin color, my eye color. I tell them learn Spanish, I don't care White people visiting Mexico speak no Spanish. Why me need to speak English only? But, I agree that I need to learn English because I'm living in America, even my kids prefer to speaking English. I came to John's class to learn, but dropped out when Amy taught. The class was different, no longer interesting. I also have to lose my weight for my daughter's Quinceañera. I dropped because one, the class is no interesting, and two I need time for my daughter's Quinceañera.

Elsa (pseudonym) is 41 years old and has lived in the US for 17 years. She graduated high school in Mexico and came to the US with her ex-husband. He worked in construction and travelled to many states for his work, including Texas, Arkansas, Ohio and Georgia. Elsa's two children, a son and a daughter, were born in the US. Elsa decided to come to the US for more opportunities for both herself and her children. To Elsa, living in Mexico was not easy and not fair. In Mexico, Elsa said that if you have no money, you cannot go to school, no matter how smart you are. When Elsa was five years old, she lost her parents. Her uncle took care of her and her younger sister and older brother. Elsa worked in her uncle's pharmacy. 'In the US, not everyone can work at a pharmacy, but in Mexico anyone can. I studied by myself reading books and asking questions to my uncle. I was 10 when I worked at his pharmacy'. When Elsa graduated high school, she dreamed of going to college but could not because of financial issues. Elsa talked to her husband about going to the US someday for more opportunities. After travelling to several states, Elsa thought that she needed a house and more people she could contact for help like friends and community members. They decided to come to Oklahoma, where the cost of living is more affordable. Her husband bought a house with Elsa, but then they divorced. Currently, Elsa is a single mom supporting two children by working as a housekeeping service provider for private houses and a part-time waitress.

Elsa came to my class in September 2016. Eva introduced Elsa to my class. They have been friends for 10 years, ever since they met at their daughters' elementary school. Elsa was an active student too, always doing her homework carefully and creatively (see Figure 4.8). Eva had taken adult ESL classes several times over the previous 10 years. She recalled that, 'John, you are the best teacher ever'. I asked why, and she said, 'your class is interesting, teach very good'.

Figure 4.8 Elsa's drawing for a self-presentation day. Her work was the most carefully drawn portrait among her peers (*pseudonym is used for Elsa)

When I returned from sick leave, Elsa was no longer present in the class. Elsa took teacher Derek's and Amy's classes, but eventually dropped out of Amy's class. She recalled that, 'Derek was very boring, doing the same thing, I thought staying home is better than wasting time in Derek's class'. Her final decision to drop out occurred when she was in Amy's class. 'Amy was a good teacher, better than Derek, but not interesting class. She needs to make her class more interesting and meaningful. I learn nothing from Amy's class'. Amy played games some days and those games were fun but not good for learning, according to Elsa. At the same time, Elsa began to think that Amy's class was a waste of time, and her daughter's quinceañera was in active preparation. Her daughter was pushing Elsa to lose weight. For Elsa, going to the gym was more meaningful than sitting in Amy's class learning nothing. 'I dropped because one, I learn nothing from Amy's class, and two, I need to lose weight for my daughter's quinceañera'.

Elsa seems to value her heritage culture and language more than other participants. When Elsa and Eva first met, Elsa recalled 'Eva's daughter was very good at speaking and writing both English and Spanish. My daughter and son understand Spanish, but are not good at writing'. Elsa actively argues against White people who push her to speak English because she lives in the US, saying, 'No you learn Spanish, I don't care when White people visit Mexico and no speak Spanish'. Elsa even said that she encountered some White racists who say that they are smarter than other people with different skin colors. She recounted, 'My skin is not my choice, God made me this way. I want to have white skin and blue eyes, but this is me'. Whenever Elsa has her children's friends visit her house, she says, 'Speak Spanish in my house'. Elsa does not want her children to lose their Spanish culture and language; it is their heritage. At the same time, she agrees that she needs to learn English because it means self-improvement in the US, opening more doors for herself and her family.

Elsa is an undocumented immigrant. Before the Trump administration, she said that she was okay to renew her driver's license in New Mexico every three years. But after the Trump administration, the Department of Motor Vehicles (DMV) office in New Mexico said 'no' to her request to renew her driver's license. She drives every day without a valid driver's license. One day, a police officer pulled her over and checked her ID. Fortunately, Elsa had her passport in her car, so the ID issue was okay, but the problem was focused on her driver's license. She showed her old driver's license to the police and said, 'I'm just about to renew my driver's license'. The police office asked Elsa about her status by asking 'legal or illegal'. Elsa said 'illegal' and waited for a stormy reaction and after that – deportation. But for some reason, the police didn't talk about it anymore, and instead asked Elsa to call a friend with a valid driver's license to come and drive the car. Her friend came, and the police officer just watched the process. Elsa arrived home okay that night in October 2017. Elsa's immigration status is on the margins, but as a Catholic, she believes 'God protects me'.

Chris' Story

I came to the US to support my family. I'm illegal. I paid $3,000 to cross the border, I climbed the fence, and walked one night to reach out a lodge in Texas, from there people gave me a ride to Tuscan, Arizona and Okla-homa City later. I paid $60 for my fake social. I came to the English class because of my probation for using fake social security card, but now I want to keep coming to the English class because I need more English.

Chris (pseudonym) is 25 years old and came to the US five years ago to support his family in Mexico. Chris crossed the border by paying $3000 to a broker. He climbed over a high fence and walked 25 hours to reach a lodge located in Texas. At the lodge, he met a group of Mexican people who gave him a ride to Tucson, Arizona. He ended up in Oklahoma City. Chris' cousin lives in Oklahoma City and has his own construction business. Chris started working at his cousin's company by driving a delivery truck, delivering big equipment and transporting lumber. Chris makes up to $1000 per week. He sends most of his money to his mother and twin sister living in Mexico. Chris has an older brother who is married and living in the US with documents. His sister also lives in the US, but is not yet documented. In his family, single children send money to his mother for support. When he is married, Chris said he might stop sending money.

Chris came to my class in September 2016. The first night, he came to me and said, 'I am on probation. I need my teacher's signature to say that I am taking an English class. Can you give me a signature?'. I reported this to my boss, who made a simple form composed of his name, class date/time and a space for my signature. Later during his interview, I learned that his probation is because he used a fake social security card. One day, a police officer pulled his car over, and the officer found the fake social security card in Chris' wallet. 'I should've not brought my fake social with me, my sister said that to me, I just forgot', Chris recalled. This incident caused him an overnight stay in jail. He paid $2000 for a bail bond and was on probation for six months. He has to pay $40 every month to the probation office and submit the English class attendance sheet. Although his first motivation to come to the class was a probation requirement, Chris was a fast learner and a bright and active student. He actively asked questions and worked well with other classmates in group work (see Figure 4.9). Chris remained when I returned after my sick leave. When Irma suggested the Sunday school idea, Chris came too, regardless of his probation requirement. He said, 'Even after my proba-tion is over, I want to keep coming. I need more English'.

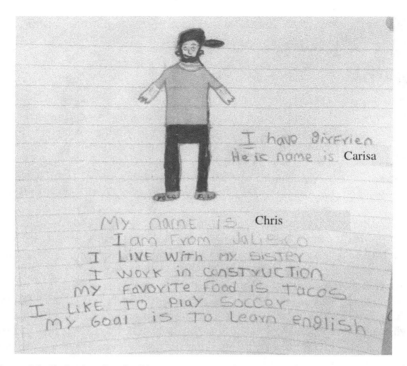

I have girfrien
He is name is Carisa

My name is Chris
I am from Jalisco
I live with my sister
I work in construction
my favorite food is tacos
I like to play soccer
my goal is to learn english

Figure 4.9 Chris' drawing for his presentation. Although his first motivation to come to the class was probation, he actively participated in the class (*pseudonyms are used for Chris and his girlfriend)

Chris' motivation to learn English was self-improvement at his place of work and family. In his job, he meets different English-speaking people every morning and must introduce himself and explain the work order for the day. He also needs to read measurements in English when he buys lumber and he needs to talk to people in the stores. Chris took those challenges as opportunities to learn English. In addition, he is dating a Mexican-American person. She does not speak Spanish. For Chris, his girlfriend is a good English teacher. Chris is planning to marry her and do the paperwork for his immigration status. Chris asked his sister who is living in Mexico to come to the US, and she said she wanted to. Teaching his sister English is another motivation for Chris to come to English class.

Unlike the other five participants, Chris never dropped out of English class. Of course, he needed the signature for his probation. However, during the interview he said, if there had been no probation requirements, he would have dropped out of Derek's and Amy's classes. 'If no probation, I would drop Derek's class, because teacher Derek is so boring, I learn nothing', he said. For Amy's class, 'I feel 50:50, if no probation, I would maybe not coming to Amy's class either. Amy speaks too fast, I don't understand. It's waste of time'. Like Irma, he prefers group work and dynamic activities to learn English. But teachers Amy and Derek didn't give any group work, and teacher Amy didn't even give a break. Chris kept coming for his probation. It seems that his body was there, but his mind was absent. When I interviewed him in summer 2017, he said he wants to keep coming even after his probation ends. The fact that he came to the Sunday schools seems to support his point (Figure 4.10).

Figure 4.10 Poster that Chris and his peers made while working together to present the history of Thanksgiving. The pilgrimage and harvesting are illustrated (*pseudonyms are used for students)

Table 4.1 Participants' characteristics and backgrounds

Name (pseudonym)	Age	Gender	Duration in the US (years)	Education	Job	English Proficiency (ACTFL OPI rating based)
Mag	27	F	4	Middle school graduate	Manufacturing drawer	Novice mid
Irma	51	F	27	Middle school graduate	Making cardboard	Intermediate low
Domingo	32	M	17	Middle school graduate	Construction	Intermediate low
Eva	42	F	10	Middle school graduate	Food preparation	Intermediate low
Elsa	41	F	17	High school graduate	Housekeeping (waitress part-time)	Intermediate mid
Chris	25	M	7	High school graduate	Construction	Intermediate low

Table 4.1 illustrates the participants' characteristics and backgrounds. Out of the six participants, five of them dropped out of their English classes. Four participants are female and two are male students. The average duration of their time living in the US is approximately 13 years.

5 Who They Are: Thematic Identity of the Six Adult English Learners

The six participants' backgrounds are foundational to this book's findings because the situatedness of the specific adult English learners (ELs) must be considered to explore their identity that foregrounds their investment factors. Upon the understanding, inductive and thematic analysis of the interview data, observational notes, survey responses and student work examples were conducted. A total of 1668 codes and 35 categories emerged; the categories were thematically mapped out (Shank, 2002). This chapter reports a thematic analysis of the six participants.

Theme 1: Family – Opportunities – 13 Years+

The data revealed that the adult Spanish-speaking ELs who want to learn English at the Center for English Literacy (CEL) have family support responsibilities, felt that there were more rewards and opportunities in the US than in their home country, which seemed to have led them to come and live in the US for more than 13 years on average.

Family support responsibility

When Domingo was 15 years old, he came to the US to support his family rather than to study for himself. He decided to stay in the US after working for a petroleum company as a valve operator. His friends who came with Domingo decided to stay and recommended Domingo also stay. After his first work trial, Domingo believed that working in the US was easier than he thought. He was paid more than the minimum wage, so he decided to stay to support his family in Mexico:

> …And then they [Domingo's friends] don't go back [to Mexico], Yeah, they stayed. Well, I started working at a petroleum company. Yeah good money. Like, I think it's the minimum wage was $6.75, they pay me like I think $10 per hour. In one week, I make like 700. You know, 700 is good money… in that time. And I, because the minimum wage was 6.75 I'm thinking. 'Yeah… oh, it's good money, it's easy job, good money. Oh,

okay, it's good for me, good opportunity. Okay, I will stay'. You know, that's why I stay to support my family in Mexico.

Chris also decided to cross the border fence to support his family in Mexico. He reported that he could make the same amount of money for working just one day in the US than he could working five days in Mexico. He said that he worried about how to support his family in Mexico, which made him to come to the US. He believed that he can make more money in the US to support his family:

> Yeah... I have to worry, I have to send the money to my mom. In Mexico, I work five days to make money, right here I work only one day for the same money. Right here for one day I make $200, in Mexico, I have to work five days to make $200, but here one day.

This family support responsibility is not only for family in Mexico, but also for immediate family members living together in the US. Domingo dreamed of pursuing his General Education Development (GED) diploma, but he put that dream on hold because supporting his wife and three children is the most important priority at this moment. Domingo said:

> ...Yeah, now we need to work and support my family... [GED is] Yeah, for future, you know..., because right now [if] I'm going to go to the school for my GED, who support my house?

This yielding of dreams due to family support responsibilities was also true with Elsa. Although Elsa always wanted to go to college, she put her dream on hold because she wanted to support her children's education first:

> I, sometime when I was sleeping in my bed, wake up in the middle of the night, because all the time in my mind is I want to come back to school. I think, why my dreams, why no go to the college, I want to go the college. But I can't. Because I am married, I have my kids [to support].

Family support responsibility for immediate family members in the US also yielded their wishes to go back to Mexico. Unlike the other five participants, Eva always wanted to go back to Mexico. Her husband said they could earn money for two to three years in the US, and then go back to Mexico. It was a condition that caused Eva to say 'yes' to his suggestion to go to the US. After three years, however, her husband and daughter requested to stay in the US, which seemed to give Eva the family support responsibility as a way of staying:

Eva: Cause they, I think that my husband said, okay we need two-three years to work [in the US], save our money, and come back [to Mexico].

I: And you agree.

Eva: Uh-huh.

I: He said, 'let's go to the US and try and come back' but you didn't go back to Mexico, right?

Eva: No. He don't want to come back and Delma [pseudonym, Eva's daughter] no come back.

Eva: Maybe only for me, everything and my family is in Mexico.

I: That's why you want to go [back to Mexico]

Eva: Uh-huh.

I: But Delma, Delma likes here more.

Eva: Yeah.

I: Your husband likes here more, too. Do you know why maybe?

Eva: Maybe, its more better to live here, more better and then I don't know.

He likes United States. He ask Delma, 'Delma, you want to come back to Mexico?', Delma said no. [So, I said] Okay, we stay here.

More rewards and opportunities

More rewards and opportunities in the US for adult Spanish-speaking ELs and their children were consistently reported throughout all six participants' interviews. For Elsa, who had a hard time supporting her own education when she was younger, US education is better and fairer, regardless of the wealth of a student's family. Elsa said:

> In United State everything is fair, free [in public schools] ... in Mexico no free school...In the United State, you lunch free in public schools... Yeah but in Mexico you need to pay for everything. Money for lunch for your kids or... for books, for uniform, for everything. If no have moneys... no money, no education. In Mexico, if you are very smart but you don't have money to go to college... you no go to college. Or if a person has parents, cause his parents have money but if you are no good student, but the parents have money, you go to the college. But in United States is different.

Mag also came to the US for a better future for her daughters. In addition to the opportunities for a better life, immediate materialistic rewards were considered as a reward and opportunity. For example, in Mexico it is hard to own a car regardless of how hard you work, but in the US, as long as you work hard, then you can own a car. Mag and Mario said that eating out at a restaurant is a very hard thing to do in Mexico, but in the US, the prices are affordable. They said that the pay for hours worked was fair in the US, and mentioned the affordability of going to a McDonald's restaurant as an example. They initially decided to cross the border with their family support responsibility. Being able to buy a car and go to a McDonald's restaurant seem to work as good evidence and a symbolic reality for their initial and ongoing decisions to come and stay in the US. Mario said:

> Yeah that's the reason I came here [helping Mario's family in Mexico] and when I came here, it's easier here at life... If you work hard, the dollar is good. You can have more things than in Mexico. In Mexico you make a little money and weekly and it was expensive. ...if you work all day in Mexico, you make a day... if you go in a MacDonald's in Mexico, one hamburger is like how many is it... like $6.00 here in the US, in Mexico you spend like $100 for one hamburger. So is very hard to get.... And, you can drive a car here, and here you work hard and maybe in six months you can buy a car. In Mexico no... no new, no old [cars]... So here is easier... yeah you can get your stuff in the US, but no in Mexico.

Living in the US 13 years+

For the adult ELs at the CEL, their family support responsibility seemed to inspire them to come to the US in the hope of more rewards and opportunities. These linkages between the two categories (responsibility and rewards) seemed to lead the participants to live in the US for more than 13 years on average. Family support needs as a thematic driving force behind adult ELs' decisions to come to the US and to invest in their learning is consistent with previous research that found supporting family needs is a reason for adult ELs' decisions to invest in English learning (Buttaro, 2002, 2004; Gault, 2003; McVay, 2004). A distinctive aspect that my book explores is the ongoing responsibility to provide family support as a deciding factor. What made them initially cross the border to support family in Mexico eventually evolved into an investment factor to learn English.

Theme 2: Physical Work – Pride – Language Barrier

Along with the dominant themes mentioned previously (family support responsibility, more rewards and opportunities in the US and living in the US for 13+ years), data revealed that the adult Spanish-speaking ELs in the CEL do physical labor jobs and at the same time they feel pride in their full-time work and collaboration experiences in the US. While working in a totally different linguistic and cultural situation to support their family, they encountered language barriers, not only at work, but also ironically with their family.

Physical labor

All six participants and their spouses worked jobs that required physical labor, such as construction (Domingo, Chris), manufacturing (Irma, Mag), housekeeping (Elsa) and food preparation (Eva). For example, Irma worked for a few months in strawberry fields, but soon after, she started working in a factory. Irma's daughter Samantha reported that Irma and her ex-husband worked in the fields first, but Irma said her first job was working in a factory. Irma said that she prefers working in a factory to other jobs. Samantha reported:

> ...And they [Irma and her ex-husband] met in Mexico. They got married and then they came to the United States because of work. They used to work in the, in the strawberry fields, potato fields, like that, all the fields. Yeah, they went to North Carolina, Oklahoma and Texas and California. So, they went everywhere. And they worked in all type of fields. And my mom's sister was settled here in Oklahoma so we came and lived with them and that's why we stayed here.

Irma didn't mention her work in the fields, but she started talking from her work experiences in a factory in Oklahoma City:

> ...Yeah, when I came over USA, my first job was in, one factory when they do bags of respiration for hospital, and I was in that place for maybe nine years in Oklahoma City. Then I work in the nursing home for maybe three years. I care people who are 60-70 years old for maybe three or four years. Then I worked in other factory where they do mattresses in Edmond, Oklahoma. Then I came to the other place, other factory, and they do bags for plants. I work in that place for four years. Then, I no more work for one year and a half. And now I work in other factory, I like the jobs only in factory. I no like other work in hotels or stores. I no like that job, only like the factories. Because when I was very young, in 16 years I work only in factories.

Pride: Full-time work and collaboration

While working physical labor jobs, the participants seem to have pride in their full-time work as they are hard workers, working for more than 10 years on average, and collaborating well with colleagues. For example, Mag felt proud of herself because she was a hard worker and made more products than her other colleagues, which made her boss happy:

> I am hard worker...My boss is happy for me. I make per day 50 [drawers]...I make, I put the reels for drawers. The night shift makes 40 boxes, they are more lazy [laugh].

This feeling of pride is derived not only from high productivity, but also from the meaningful role that the participants have in their work. For example, Irma worked as an English 'translator' between her colleagues and her boss for work orders and directions, which made her very proud of herself. Sometimes, Irma's colleagues asked her where she learned English, which heightened her self-confidence as she was perceived as having high English proficiency:

> Yeah, mistake... [when my colleagues make mistakes, they] ...only shake that cardboard and separate. So, when the supervisor, he calls me. 'Irma tell her [Irma's colleague] this, Irma, can do this, yeah, can you do this?' And, I say 'of course'. And I feel better. He [her boss] understands me. He understand and I feel better. And the lady [colleagues] say, 'where you learn English?'. And I say 'well, I have my teacher, my teacher is John and he is good teacher'. 'Oh really? I want to go'. 'Okay, wait, wait'.

On average, the participants have had a full-time job in the US for 11 years, which seems to give them a feeling of pride. Eva has worked for 10 years at her restaurant, Elsa for 10 years in housekeeping, Domingo for 17 years in construction, Irma for 16 years in manufacturing and Chris for 7 years in construction. Their pride in working full-time and collaborating with their colleagues seemed to be derived from the fact that that they 'support' their family and learn through this support. Domingo recounted this relational feeling between family support and pride in working full time with a determined tone, saying, 'Yeah, now. You know, now we need to work and now but support my family'. Elsa recounted that she feels good and proud that she supports her two children with her housekeeping work and her part-time waitress job. She said that she learns a lot from her work:

> I learned more when I was working in the restaurant, I like it because sometimes prep, prepare, sometime help out. But my work is busy, cleaning the tables. And I like it, because I practice my English with the customers.

Language barrier at work, family and community

The six participants encountered language barriers at work and ironically with family too.

At work

First, language barriers at work appeared in dynamic and different forms for each participant, such as their lack in reading construction maps (Domingo), talking to people in stores when buying lumber

(Chris), understanding colleagues' and boss' directions (Eva and Elsa), answering phone calls from bosses (Mag) and advocating for themselves by explaining their opinions on unwilling/incapable work (Irma). Those barriers seemed to give them a certain degree of oppressed feelings and discriminatory treatment at their job. For example, Irma recalled that when she spoke very little English, her boss gave her an order to carry heavy boxes. The boxes were too heavy for Irma to carry, so she wanted to say no and list the reasons why she could not carry them, but she was unable to persuasively convince her boss. So, she carried the boxes and hurt herself. Irma saw that her boss went to other people asking them to carry the boxes too, but their English was good enough to say no, so they didn't carry the boxes. People with good English did 'light' jobs, such as working on a computer or cutting paper. It seemed unfair to Irma, because they were paid the same, regardless of if they worked with heavy boxes or light paper:

> [if your English is not good] ... more jobs and heavy. Because I think when we no speak English, they give the jobs more heavy. For example, in my other job, they told me to pick up heavy box, deep box. He said, go and pick it up Irma. And I say it's too heavy for me somebody can help. He said, no you can do it, you can do it for yourself. Yeah, [my English was] no good, not much. [so I carried the box]. But the other people speak good English, they say, no I don't want to, somebody can do that, not me. And the boss went for other people, and the other people can't say anything, but have to carry box. When other people speak English more better, they do something else. Like, go see that computer, go see that... papers, or cut paper. We get paid same money. It's not fair.

Mag experiences language barriers when she gets a phone call from her boss. Speaking over the phone gives another layer of language barrier to Mag:

> Sometimes it was hard for me to speak English by phone. Something like my boss call me and, I think, 'oh I don't understand what he say', I just say yes, yes [although I don't understand].

In family

Within family, language barriers have been built, especially with the children of married participants and with the significant other of single participants. For example, Domingo's sons talk to their mother in English, but talk to Domingo in Spanish. Domingo sometimes doesn't understand the conversations between his children and his wife. Domingo's sons brought English books they read for schoolwork and asked Domingo questions, but Domingo didn't know how to read the books, so he told them to talk to Samantha, which made him feel bad, but also motivated him to learn more English:

> Well, right now, because my kids, when it's, how to read English. And the school send that [English books] to me. So, when reading written English, okay, you say simply like, 'the cat is crying' [in the English books]. Then, my son asked me, 'the cat is mad?' My son asked me, 'What did he say?' Then I said, 'I don't know, ask your mom'. My kids wouldn't [study with me], I don't know how to read this book.

This language barrier with children was consistent with Eva and Elsa and their teenaged children. Whenever their children's friends visited their houses, Eva and Elsa told them to speak Spanish, but the children still spoke English. Elsa recalled one day that her nephews came to her house and spoke English by arguing against Elsa's 'policy' to speak Spanish in her house:

> And for me sometime I think 'oh, it's fine cause I want my kids learn, speak Spanish, don't forget Spanish'. But, the friends of my daughter don't talk Spanish, No speak Spanish, [so I asked] 'you don't want speak Spanish?'... And sometimes the friends come into my home. I said 'okay, in my home talk in Spanish. Everybody'... My daughter talks in Spanish and then my home, but the little kids [nephews], only talk in English.

The children's reason was that they live in America, so they want to speak English. And the children said that they only want to speak Spanish with their grandparents:

> I said, you come into my home, I said you need to talk in Spanish in my home. The little kid [Elsa's nephew] said 'why, I live in America'. I said 'so, you come into my home, you talk in Spanish'. He said 'okay, only to grandma I talk in Spanish. You are not grandma'.

Elsa's primary reason to have her children speak Spanish was that she wants them to retain their heritage. As with the other participants, Elsa likes to practice English at work with her colleagues, but she wants to talk in Spanish with her children:

> And I say it's good for me, because sometimes I talk to my kids, and I say speak English for me because I want to learn. But with my kids, no, I want to speak Spanish.

This conflict over viewpoints between heritage culture and language might work as a behind-the-scenes factor of language barrier issues within families. There is a silent battle between 'keeping heritage values' and the reasoning of 'I want to speak English because I live in America'. Ironically, Elsa dislikes the reason of 'living in America' for speaking English, but at the same time she agrees with that justification because she admits that she needs English to live in the US. Elsa recounted:

> Because I live in America and more the people speak English and I have problems when I want to talk to somebody and English open many doors, like I said for work or everything.

On the other hand, as a single person, Chris experienced this language barrier with his girlfriend. His girlfriend is Latin American, but she doesn't speak Spanish. It is good for Chris to practice English with her, but at the same time misunderstanding and miscommunication sometimes seem to frustrate him:

> I got my girlfriend and my girlfriend she don't speak Spanish. When my girlfriend tell me something sometimes I don't understand. Yeah…. [then I said] Yeah, tell me one more time.

In the community

Language barriers also occurred within the participants' communities, especially when they need to seek medical treatment for either themselves or their family members. Irma struggled with the language barrier at the emergency room when she couldn't speak with the doctors and her two young daughters had to translate about their father's death. Elsa also recalled that her daughter once had a stomachache, so they went to an emergency room. Elsa's English proficiency is quite good and she has no problem with daily communications. However, she recalled that she could not think of any English words that night because she was so nervous and worried about her daughter. Those affective aspects seemed to rapidly build the language barrier that night, where she recalled that her daughter didn't want to help translate:

> And sometime when my kids don't want to help me [by translating], because I can't speak very good English, and when I was nervous, I saw my daughter. I usually can speak my English long time. But, the last time, when my daughter was sick, I went to emergency room and I was in front of the nurse. I hear, the nurse saying, 'can I help you?', and I say, 'yes' and I saw my daughter and I can't speak because my English was gone. And, I thought 'oh my gosh my English is gone because I was nervous'.

After the emergency room visit, Elsa and her daughter talked about why her daughter didn't help Elsa by translating between the doctors. This community-based language barrier seems subtly related to another layer of language-based barrier within Elsa's family, but at the same time it gave Elsa the desire to learn English:

> And after I talked to my daughter, I said 'you didn't help me'. My daughter said 'mom, he [a hospital staff] asked you if you want an emergency room and you say yes', and she say 'ah, the emergency room is this way'. And I say, 'okay thank you'. And after I laugh with my daughter and I took my daughter and I said, 'you didn't help me'. And sometimes I ask my son and my daughter 'what is that one?' My daughter said, 'I don't know, mom you help me. I don't know. You need to go to school where you learn English' and my daughter said, 'you're mean mom'. And, okay I go to my English class. Cause I want to learn, cause sometimes my kids don't help me.

In addition to her work, Mag also encountered language barriers in medical needs for her son. Recall that Mag's reason for coming to the EL class was that she needed more English to be a candidate for a job promotion – working inside. In addition to the work-based language barrier issues, Mag experienced language barriers at hospital when her son had an earache. When Mag's husband is able to come with her, they are okay with talking with the doctors. But in other cases, Mag struggles to communicate with the doctors. A translation service is available, but Mag wants to talk directly to the doctors:

> At appointment, the doctor, I don't understand… When I have appointments when I go to the doctor. I don't understand what they say. The doctors or you try to get some papers for the kids and you don't speak English, you feel like embarrassed. My kid has the tubes in his ears. The tubes in ears and the doctor speaks, you don't understand. They put the tube maybe last year, because my son has water in his ears. Doctors put something and now is okay. It was hard for me when I had some appointments. Some place my husband can go with me. Sometimes somebody speak Spanish in the clinic. But where they make a test for the ear, they don't speak Spanish.

Although Chris has no children, he indirectly experienced this medical service-based language barrier with his friend. One day, Chris witnessed that his friend was injured while he played soccer. They went to an emergency room. Chris saw that his friend could not communicate with the doctors about his broken leg. Chris imagined that he could be in that situation, because he works at construction and sometimes plays soccer. For Chris, imagining his situatedness seems to give him the sense of language barriers at hospitals:

I: You said, I want to learn English for Hospital, an example?
Chris: If I break my leg, yeah I have to pick a Spanish one then.

I: If? You break your leg before?

Chris: No. No. But I see other guys, my friend he broke his leg. And I go see at the hospital, and the doctor he was say something to him and he don't know what he said.

I: What happened to him? He fell down?

Chris: In the game of football, football game.

I: Oh really, he played a football game and broke…

Chris: Yeah.

I: So you imagined that, oh maybe when I break my leg I want to go to the hospital'?

Chris: Yeah, I want to learn English for communication with the doctor.

Theme 3: Desire to Learn English – Community Access – Christianity

For the participants, the diverse forms of language barriers seemed to trigger a strong desire to learn English, which led them to search for community access to learn English. Along the way, Christianity seems to play a role in the community access category as a part of their identity/culture. The desire to learn English emerged dynamically across all six participants' interviews and observation field notes.

Desire to learn English

All six participants said that they always wanted to learn English:

'I always want to learn English' (Mag).

'I want to learn English better' (Domingo).

'I want to learn more English and perfection my English' (Irma).

'Um, No…. [to a question 'have you felt that I don't want to learn English?'] …, because all the time I need English' (Eva).

'I go to my English class. Cause I want to learn' (Elsa).

'I never say that [I don't want to learn English], I come, because I want to learn English' (Chris).

During the interviews, all the participants asked me about an English expression for the idea they wanted to say by asking, 'How do you say this in English?'. For example, Irma asked me about the difference between 'teach' and 'learn'. Domingo asked me to correct his pronunciation of the word 'important' (he pronounces it /import/). Eva asked me about the difference between 'prep' and 'prepare'. Elsa asked me the difference between 'lose' and 'lost'. Lastly, Chris asked me how to greet an American customer in the morning for his work. We talked about the expression 'I am here to concrete the pool', and Chris applied it by saying, 'How about saying – I am the concrete guy, tell me where please'.

Community access

These desires to learn English seem to motivate them to pursue community access to learn English for their life needs. Their community access already existed, such as access to churches, neighborhoods and friends. The importance of dynamic community access emerged from their interview data. For Irma and Domingo, their Spanish-speaking pastor recommended going to an adult English class at the church located in their community. Irma recalled that:

> Oh, because my pastor say 'Irma somebody come and learn English' and I said 'really', and he say 'yeah you want to come?' Yeah, yeah, I say 'yeah and I can'.

On the other hand, Mag, Chris and Eva first came to the class by seeing the church sign saying that there is a free English class (Figure 5.1):

Chris: I pass by here and I see the...
I: Sign.
Chris: Sign.
I: You live close to here?
Chris: Yeah I live close.

Elsa's case was a bit different, but her community access to friends (Eva) encouraged her to come to the class. Elsa recounted that, '[I come] ... Cause Eva told me the English class'. This community access was not only highlighted for English learning needs, but also for students' diverse life needs such as help for medical situations, housing and even for crossing the border. For example, after living in different states, Elsa decided

Figure 5.1 Church sign for free English class – students first came to their English classes on seeing this sign, including Mag, Chris and Eva

to come to Oklahoma because houses in Oklahoma were cheaper, and there were relatively less people that she could talk to in Spanish in Georgia when she was there. She expected to meet more Spanish-speaking people in Oklahoma:

> But, in Georgia everything was more expensive than Oklahoma. He and I wanted to buy home and he said Georgia was more expensive than Oklahoma. When I was living in Georgia, I didn't have any family or friends, or people from Mexico. I don't have anybody who can help me. And sometimes he worked in Florida and North Carolina and South Carolina, I am myself with my two kids in Georgia. And he said no, let's move to Oklahoma where homes are more cheaper. More Spanish-speaking people. And I said, okay. And after he saved money and we buy, gosh, a home.

Irma recounted that in life, there are many moments to ask help from others. Thus, she said community access is important. It seems that learning English is important to her as a means of accessing communities she needs:

> Yeah and that time what I see is important for me learn English. Me no English because you know the life got a lot of moments, importance. When we need to talk and understand, if we know English, we can ask, 'oh man, can you help me, can you help me?' I looking for anybody. Yeah, it's why I need [English and community].

Lastly, the fact that Chris was able to cross the border by paying $3000 to brokers showed his community access to some degree too. He came to the US with a couple of men. He walked 24–25 hours to reach a big house in Texas, where he met a group of Mexican people. They gave him rides to the next spots. This seems to be another form of community access in this particular sociopolitical context:

> I pay another people [brokers] to bring me right here [the US]. I gave them, the people bringing me right here $3,000. I pass right here the guys, the Mexican guys they were, right here in his car. When I was in the car I go to Phoenix, Arizona. And when I was in Phoenix, Arizona, some Mexican guys from right here, from Tulsa. They go over there, pick me up. And bring me to Oklahoma, yeah.

Christianity

Christianity is another category that emerged in all six participants' data, which seems to be a part of the Spanish-speaking adult ELs' identity/culture. Irma is a pastor's granddaughter. Domingo became a Christian after he experienced his medical situation five years previously.

Domingo, Samantha and Irma recounted that their prayers were answered to cure Domingo of his liver disease. Mag is a Catholic as are Eva and Elsa. Another point to recall is that the class venue was a local Protestant church. Given the nature of this context, the CEL sends their teachers to satellite locations to teach, including churches, elementary schools and factory cafeterias. However, in this particular case, Christianity seems to interplay within the community access category.

Theme 4: Family Support My Learning – Discursive Study Strategies

For their English-learning journey, all six participants reported that their family supported their English learning, and they seemed to develop their own discursive study strategies toward how to effectively learn, practice and master the English language.

Family support my learning

Domingo sometimes asked his wife Samantha English questions and she helped him. For Mag, her husband Mario supported her going to English classes at night by taking care of her children while she was away studying. Mario said:

> Yeah I always tell her [Mag] go, go. Yeah I don't have a problem. I might take her and the kids here [English class]. I all the time I tell her you need to go, learn.

For Elsa, her two children gave her a flyer that said there was an English class for adult learners:

> My son or my daughter, I don't remember when, bring the paper [class advertisement] and say 'mom, the teacher put this paper and next week start English class for, ESL class for adults'. Class was in the afternoon. And I say, 'oh let me take, oh it's 6pm in the school, okay'. And when I start my English class, my bad dreams disappear.

For Eva, she had a time conflict between her EL class and her babysitting responsibility for her friend. But Eva said that she could ask her daughter Delma to take care of the baby, and Eva could go to learn English. This is another form of family support for her English learning:

> Sometimes I can go, for my friend's babysitting, I can ask Delma [Eva's daughter], 'Delma, you take care of this baby, I go to class'.

In addition, as a teacher, I recalled that the participants' family members sometimes visited their English classes to support them. Samantha came to support Irma and Domingo, and she helped me as a translator. Eli (Samantha's sister) also came a few days to support Irma. Delma visited once to support Eva by translating as necessary. Family support for the participants' English learning seemed to be based on the previous themes, such as language barriers with family, desire to learn English and community access.

Discursive study strategies

The participants seem to have their own discursive study strategies that they use, hope to apply and adapt in their lives. These include work, family and community. For example, Domingo believes that 'understanding the idea' behind the sounds and letters is more important to learning a second language (L2). During the interview, he showed me the importance of ideas by teaching me a Spanish word, 'rojo (red)'. He first just spoke the sound without any other meaning association, and later he said 'rojo' and pointed out a red chair in the room:

Domingo: You know the peoples got an idea of what you're talking [about].

I: Idea. You kept saying idea. So, is idea important for you?

Domingo: Sure, because I speak Spanish, I talk some things in Spanish, and you do not have an idea what I am talking about. For example, rojo [just spoke the word in the air]

I: I have no idea.

Domingo: What is rojo? This is the color [pointing out a red chair in the room]

I: Okay.

Domingo: Rojo is red, you know. Do you see it, the color. This, you have idea what I am talking about it, right?

I: Mhmm. Mhmm.

Domingo: This is what you're talking about.

I: Idea is important for you.

Domingo: Yeah, it [idea] is very important.

To Domingo, learning with more examples and practicing with those examples helps him better understand the ideas:

Yeah, practice the example is important. How to make sentence, have an idea. Right, because when you put your sentence practice, you have an idea, and other people got the idea how to make sentence. For example, I remember the sentences, apartments [a textbook topic was about apartment housing] and you write it [on the whiteboard]. They, the apartments, and then people write it same, copy you, do practice examples. Right.

The importance of practice was also echoed in Mag's study strategy. Mag said she likes to repeat and practice to learn English:

> [I like] Repeat, repeat, repeat... I like how you teach because you make questions and they [classmates] answer. If they don't speak, you'll repeat it again and so we practice. I like practice.

Mag also watches a TV show with English subtitles to learn: 'And I try to watch TV in English and I put the captions because I can, I can write down more. I understand more if I read or write down the speak'. Likewise, Elsa likes to practice her English. But Elsa's strategy has a different color, she likes to practice English with the White customers visiting her restaurant:

> I like, because I practice my English with the customers. And they [customers] say 'hi, how are you?, Uh-huh, I don't see you for long time, I think you don't work anymore here'. And I say 'yes, I was working, I work in the back, in the kitchen something'. And I practice my English and I like talk to the people. I go to start talking more in the restaurant, because I see White people. More the customers is White people and talk English, English, English. I need practice my English.

It seems that all the participants take their real-life situations as learning opportunities, whether it is their job or life-related events such as shopping at stores. For instance, Elsa said that she successfully communicated with an American shopper at Walmart using English when she needed to buy grape juice for her daughter's quinceañera. Elsa used paraphrasing techniques and rewording strategies:

> I was, before the Quinceañera for my daughter, I can't find the welch juice. I ask some lady, 'excuse me I need help' and they said 'yes, yes ma'am'. And I say um, 'I don't know what I can find, bottle similar the cider, but cider is juice, the grape, it's no wine, I say' and she said 'oh I know, say what do you want, come on' and 'I, oh thank you so much'. Yeah and I say, and I ask 'what is that name, next time I know it'. They say welch juice.

Eva sometimes asks a conversation partner to slow down their English speaking so she can understand, which seems to be a good communication/English learning strategy:

> Cause I oh, my English. Or sometimes, people talk very fast and I say 'um, I'm sorry but I don't understand. Can you tell me more slow please, because my English is not good but I think you speak very fast for me. Can you speak more slowly for me?' And then people tell 'okay, okay'.

Eva and Elsa both agree that this 'slowing down' strategy works for them when they speak with their children's teachers or doctors, and when they understand, they feel happy. However, they said they don't want to ask their colleagues or boss at work to slow down their speech. It seems that they don't want to give their work colleagues the wrong or negative impression. This point seems to illustrate that they use different strategies for different sociopolitical contexts, which seems consistent with Norton (2012)'s argument that emphasizes the interrelations between language learning and power relations with interlocutors:

> I know, I say [could you slow down please?] maybe a lot in the store, maybe when I go to doctor. [saying] I don't know, my English no good. And they are okay. But for my work, I don't know, it's scary [to ask slow down].

Lastly, for classroom activities, the participants reported that they prefer using more dynamic strategies to learn English than just sitting and writing, such as group work, standing up and discussing, and presenting with pictures/drawings. For example, Chris pointed out that he likes to share ideas with his peers in group work:

> I like work in group, like with my friends and doing something and stand up... And read to other people.

Irma also recounted that she prefers group work, especially because the instructor can monitor students' English output and give feedback:

> When you make a little groups and you [instructor] come, does you walk around everybody and you hear how I pronounce my English and you see how other people pronounce their English and you say no, no, no like that you correcting everybody and we feel better because somebody is interest, interest, interest for my English.

Thematic Characteristics of Adult ELs

Participants' dynamic characteristics of family support responsibility seem to have led them to decide to come to the US many years ago. Their feeling of gaining more rewards and opportunities in the US seems to be with them before crossing the border and seems to be reinforced through their lives in the US, thus on average the participants have lived in the US for 13+ years. To support their family both in the US and Mexico, they have all been a physical laborer. At the same time, they feel pride in their full-time work and collaboration with other colleagues. Along the way, the participants encountered language barriers in their work, family and community, all of which seems to give them a strong desire to learn English. Their desire led them to pursue community access to learn English, have their family support for their English learning and develop their own discursive study strategies. Christianity seems to work as a community access window in the big picture of who they are. Figure 5.2 illustrates the relationships of these themes.

In Figure 5.2, family support responsibility and more rewards/opportunities in the US are at the top to represent the participants' initial motivational factors for their decisions to cross the border. The thick box binding the two illustrates the interrelatedness of the two in the students' minds before and after crossing the border. The arrow connecting family support responsibility with physical labor shows the probable causal relationship. In addition, the full-time work and collaboration pride category seems to emerge simultaneously when the participants did physical labor. Thus, it is connected with a solid line without any directional arrows. The arrows from physical labor and full-time work and collaboration pride toward language barriers at work, family and community illustrate that those two categories probably worked as a causing factor to the build-up of language barriers at work, family and community. On the right side, another arrow starts from more rewards/opportunities in the US to living in the US for 13+ years by showing the probable causal relation. While living in the US for such a long time, the participants recognized language barriers at work, family and community. Starting from the barriers, an

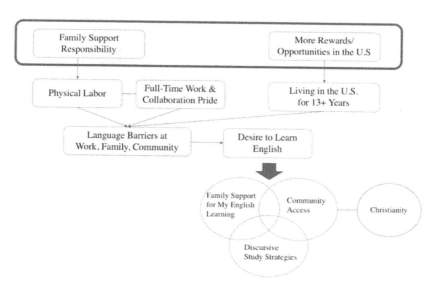

Figure 5.2 Map of the adult Spanish-speaking English learners at the CEL

arrow is connected to their desire to learn English, where three different but intertwined English learning systems/journeys/quests start from factors such as family support for my English learning, community access and discursive study strategies. Christianity seems to connect with the community access aspect in this holistic map of who the adult ELs are.

Discussion about the Thematic Identity of Six Participants

Multifacetedness and fluidity

The lives of adult ELs at the CEL are multifaceted, complex and fluid based on their specific and ever-changing situatedness. Specifically, although all participants share the dominant themes of family support responsibilities, more rewards in the US and language barriers at work, family and community, the specific characteristics of each category are diverse. For example, while one of Domingo's rewards for coming to the US was monetary compensation, it seems that Elsa's and Eva's rewards in the US were opportunities for education and jobs for their children. Likewise, the participants' detailed components in their lives seem multifaceted and dynamic. This finding seems consistent with the multifaceted nature of language learning argued by Darvin and Norton (2015) and the Douglas Fir Group (2016).

Desire to invest

Adult ELs' desire to invest in learning English seemed high when they initially came to classes. Their desire to learn English seems based on the intertwined influences from six categories such as family support responsibility, more rewards/opportunities in the US, living in the US for 13+ years, language barriers at work, family and community while they work physical labor and they feel pride in their full-time work and collaboration. This finding is consistent with previous research findings that adult ELs, in general, have high motivation to learn English (Bernat, 2004; Derwing, 2003; Hyman, 2002; Valentine, 1990). However, high motivation does not guarantee actual implementation all the time (Norton, 2012). Norton (1997, 2012) pointed out that an actual investment in learning English can be implemented when students take real action, and its constructs include ideology, identity and capital. The fact that adult ELs in this book dropped out, despite their high motivation, will be discussed along with Norton's investment framework in Chapter 6.

Multiple roles of family

Lastly, it seems that family plays multiple roles in the adult ELs' English learning journey in initiating, supporting and sometimes constraining/intimidating factors. First, it seems that the family of the adult EL helps initiate their English learning based on the language barriers they encounter within their family. The frustrations include moments when they cannot read an English book for their children (Domingo), when a girlfriend doesn't know Spanish (Chris) and children who speak English at home (Eva, Elsa). In addition to their contribution to initiating learning, their family also supports their English learning in multiple ways. For example, Mario, Mag's husband, helped Mag's English learning by taking care of their children while Mag studied. Elsa's children showed her an English as a second language (ESL) class flyer. Eva's daughter was willing to support Eva's babysitting duty when Eva wanted to go to her EL class. And many family members physically visited their English classrooms and stayed to support translating as necessary (Irma, Domingo, Eva). Nonetheless, family brings a constraining aspect to the adult ELs' English learning journey. Their family sometimes required the learners to take care of family issues and events by subtracting from their investment in learning English such as taking care of children (Mag) and preparing for quinceañera (Eva, Elsa). Having conflicts over their identity roles (an EL student vs. a parent) seems consistent with Gordon (2004), Norton-Peirce (1995) and Skilton-Sylvester (2002) who found that adult ELs struggled with and experienced their identity role negotiation while pursuing English learning.

Also, intimidating aspects were reported from family, such as when their children told them not to translate but go ahead and learn English (Eva, Elsa); when her husband asked her to attend Bible study although she seemed to want to go to her English class (Mag); and when his girlfriend said something too fast in English, thus he stayed silent and asked for clarification (Chris). This finding about the family's two different roles (support and challenge) is consistent with McVay (2004) who pointed out that family can both support and challenge an adult EL's learning, but more weight is on support. This book's findings provides another layer to the specific characteristics of family as a challenge. While McVay (2004) pointed out that collecting children from school can be a challenge, so can quinceañera, Bible study requirements and conversation with family. The challenges seem to be transferred as another motivating factor later (e.g. Chris wanted to communicate with his girlfriend better, and Domingo wanted to read the English book better to his children). Connections between family-based challenges and motivation are recursive.

Adult ELs' backgrounds are as complex as the nature of L2 learning; while their initial motivation to learn English was based on multiple background-based factors, family played multiple roles in the adult ELs' journey. ESL stakeholders should be aware of multifaceted motivational factors when developing curriculum and instruction.

6 What Drives Investment

Theme 5: Superación – Job Needs – Desire to Communicate

The thematic analysis of the interview data revealed that the adults invest mainly for their superación (a Spanish word meaning self-improvement or self-actualization), dynamic job needs: apply-work-promotion-avoid exploitation, and because they have a desire to communicate with other people on many occasions.

Superación

The most dominant finding was that the adult English learners (ELs) at the Center for English Literacy (CEL) want to invest in learning English for their superación. The detailed shapes and colors of each individual's superación were different, but this feeling was strongly shared among all six participants. For example, Mag reported that she wants to learn English mainly because she wants to be a better person:

> I don't know how to say English, Superación... Like, I don't want to stay on this level. I need to learn English so I am gonna be on the next level. So I want to learn English so I become, better person.

This desire to become a better person was also echoed by Eva. To Eva, becoming a better person, for her superación, specifically seems to mean becoming a 'fast' (fluent) speaker and listener of the English language. When I asked Eva her number one reason for wanting to learn English, she pointed out these two concepts – becoming a better person and a fast speaker:

> [My number one reason for learning English is] ...Talking English, for, maybe for talking to other people. Me want to talk more fast, more fast understand... I think if you speak more English, it's more better for you. Now you say, more better person.

As illustrated by Mag and Eva, the overarching notion of superación seems to be 'becoming a better person', which was thematically shared among all six participants. However, the details of what superación in reality means are idiosyncratically different for each individual. For example, Domingo reported that, to him, superación means helping his children with their schoolwork, life and hopes for the future through learning English. Recall that Domingo struggled when his children asked him to read English books. Domingo was not able to read them, so he sent his children to their mother:

> [Why] Learn English. Well, right now, because my kids, when it's, you know, how to read English. And the school send that [kid's reading assignment] to me then... So, when reading written English,... [my son asked me] 'What did he [a character in the book] say?' [And I said] 'I don't know, ask your mom'.

For Domingo, this incident seemed to mean much more than just the ability to read. Rather, it means the lack of superación. This lack of superación is limited by, and can be achieved through, learning English. When I asked Domingo what learning English meant to him, he recounted this superación aspect of being able to read English books and talk to his children in English. Beyond reading books, Domingo said that supporting his children's hopes by helping them and giving them advice in English was a central part of his superación. Domingo recounted that his desire to pass the General Education Development (GED) test was also in the same vein, to give hope to his children:

I: What is English for you?

Domingo: I think we need to help my kids because my kids will need that opportunity. When my kid, we need to push, you know, more, more education. More school maybe. And the GED when they get. My kid is, to the push [for achievement/development]. You know, like, right now it's more, my hope to my kids is more important than me right now.

I: Have more opportunity.

Domingo: Yeah, [my kids] have more opportunity.

I: By English?

Domingo: Mhmm [Yes], by learning English.

I: And you don't feel good about that [when Domingo can't read the English books for his kids]. So you feel, 'okay, I want to learn English'.

Domingo: I want to learn English better.

I: Because?

Domingo: Because I want to tell him [his son] what he [a character in the book] say.

I: So, you said that and that's my number one reason [to learn English], is that right?

Domingo: Yes.

I: Because before, for example, Superación, for GED is for you, right, not for your children. Is that right? Maybe passing GED is good for you or good for your children?

Domingo: Well, right now, it's for my children's hope, to him.

I: Yeah, yeah, true. Eloy (pseudonym, Domingo's son), for example.

Domingo: For example, Eloy. And, the school. Right, is why we need, is written English for me help him.

For Irma, superación meant protecting her children. The hardship that Irma experienced the night that her husband passed away 18 years ago, when her two young daughters translated between the doctor and Irma, seemed to give Irma a strong goal of protecting her children by learning English. When I asked Irma what she would like to do if her English were perfect now, she recounted the importance of protecting her kids:

I: For now then, if your English is perfect, what do you want to do?

Irma: Well, now, I think, say okay I'm right here, my daughters can go over there, I can say my daughter go over there and put in the place of safety. And I ask, the doctor and I know I go ask with my daughters about their dad, I think now is more better, like you know, because that was 18 years ago. I think my English now is better than that time.

I: So, now, for still you said if your English is perfect now, then you want to still protect your daughters.

Irma: Protect my daughters. Uh-huh [Yes], because in that time I didn't have my brothers. Right now because now I have three brothers right here in Oklahoma. But in that 18 years ago, me was only by myself. Only myself and my two daughters. So.

I: But now you have three brothers here so it is good for you… or?

Irma: Yeah, it's good, more better for me.

I: Okay. Then, so still you want to protect your daughters and that is your Superación.

Irma: Yeah.

I: And for that you need English.

Irma: Yeah, Superación for better life, [and] protect my children.

For Elsa, superación seems to be to continue her education, specifically to go to college in the US. However, Elsa has put her dream to go to college on hold because she has had to support her two children by herself. Elsa's dream to go to college and the fact that she couldn't do so for years showed up to her as a nightmare whenever she slept. Elsa recalled that when she continued her education by attending a local English as a second language (ESL) class, that nightmare disappeared. With this experience, Elsa always advises her daughter to 'follow your dreams. If you don't follow your dreams, your dreams follow you':

> And my dream, all the time it was, I want to go to college. But I can't go. When I live in United States after marriage, I have bad dreams [nightmares]. I was in my dreams, I was a student. Oh my gosh, the test paper was white and the teacher say. 'Take your test' and I was nervous cause no study for my test. Oh my gosh, it's [the test paper] in white, I don't have the answers. And I wake up. It's because I think all the time in my mind, I say I want to go to college. Oh my gosh, because it was my dream. Now my daughter she's good. My daughter, she has dreams and she say 'I want to study for lawyer mom'. For lawyer, and I say, 'Okay. You follow your dreams. If you don't follow your dreams, your dreams follow you'. My dreams follow me. Because before I had bad dreams and wake up and I was sad. I understand it's because other time I want to go to the college but I can't go. My bad dreams disappear after I start English class in United State.

For Chris, superación seems to mean being capable of talking to other people at work, such as his boss and the people at the stores where he buys materials for his work, and being able to understand and talk to his girlfriend. Although he initially came to the English language class to fulfil his probation requirement, Chris said that he wants to keep coming to learn English even after his probation ends.

Chris: Yeah two more months [to finish probation] and that's it.
I: That's good, good. So, but you said, 'okay that [probation] was maybe why you started English class, but you want to still, after probation finished, but you said you still want to come right?
Chris: Yeah I want to come.
I: So why do you want to learn English Chris?
Chris: Because in my work, I have to know English because I have to go to a store and get stuff for work. And the stores, it's like only English. And, I got my girlfriend and my girlfriend she don't speak Spanish.

To achieve his goals to be able to communicate for his work and with his girlfriend, Chris also picked 'education' as a synonym of superación as his number one reason for learning English. Chris related the education goal to an incident in the past when he remained quiet with his boss while communicating in English. Chris didn't want to stay silent. He wanted to communicate, which as another facet of his decision-making factors, seemed to lead him to put education as his top reason to learn English:

I: So education is number one [reason to learn English], can you tell me a little bit more about that?

Chris: Education.

I: Mm hmm.

Chris: For when, for the other people tried to talk to me. But, I stay quiet.

I: Other people in town, in the city?

Chris: In the city yeah. When I go to a job, the superintendent is, she don't know Spanish and when she tell me something in English, I stay quite.

I: You don't want be quite.

Chris: No. But right now... yeah. Right now I know how [to communicate in English]. Yeah, I am more better. Education for talk and communicate better.

Like Chris' case, it seems that another layer of the importance of superación appears when the participants felt embarrassed by staying quiet although they wanted to say something back to English speakers. For example, when a customer said 'Hi' to Eva, though Eva felt that she could take that time to practice her English and communicate, she ended up saying nothing and left the situation by saying 'okay, bye, I busy'. It seems that Eva didn't want to be silent, she wanted to talk and listen to communicate fluently in English. This incident seems to illustrate that her superación was challenged, which led her to set up a new goal:

> The customers, yeah sometime they come with friend and the customer say 'Hi how are you? I say, 'ah good'. Maybe somebody can talk more, more conversation. But, I said 'uh, okay I busy. I go on'. ... I no practice. The people ask me question in English. Sometime they talk to me, 'how are you?' but, I said 'Okay, bye, I busy'.

This hesitation and giving up a real desire to communicate were also reported by Irma. Whereas Eva's signal for escaping an English conversation was 'Okay, bye, I busy', Irma's signal was 'never mind'. Irma seemed to have a strong desire to communicate with other people using English, but sometimes she ended up escaping the situation, which made her feel bad about her superación. Irma recalled these 'escaping' and 'hurting her superación' moments when she tried to learn about products at a mall:

Irma: Oh, maybe when I see good deal opportunities in a shopping mall. When the people said, 'I have this for sale, but this got, this and this problem'. And I say 'what is problem about that thing?' And they say, 'it's a good, cheaper, but the problem is this and this'. And I say 'what's the problem? I don't, can't understand what is the problem'. And the person say, 'it's good opportunity for a little bit money'. But I want to understand the problem. It is why when I say, 'oh I need more English, because if I can understand that I can take that one back'. But, I don't understand, yeah I don't know what happened with that. So with that person when I go same appointment and I say I understand a little bit but not all of it. I understand a little bit but, I ask about this and I can understand more.

I: That makes sense.

Irma: Yeah and I can, you know, people, talk and talk and talk. No because I don't know how to say that, so I said 'never mind'.

I: You want to talk but maybe you don't know how to, so you don't talk?

Irma: Yeah, and I say 'never mind, bye'.

I: That doesn't look good... right.

Irma: No, that's not good.

I: Because you want to talk right?

Irma: Yeah, because I like to talk.

While the shapes and characteristics are different, the participants' number one reason to invest in English learning seems to be their superación, in other words, becoming a better person. This finding is consistent with Dewey's (1903) self-actualization notion that emphasized the importance of self-growing through education based on an individual's discursive goals and needs. The adult ELs in the CEL seem to have a strong desire for self-actualization in the US, where they have realized that English proficiency is very necessary to achieve goals like becoming a better person at work (Mag), being able to speak quickly and listen (Eva), being able to help with their children's English reading assignments and advise them in the future (Domingo), protecting their children (Irma), continuing education by following dreams (Elsa), being able to talk to people in stores and with a girlfriend (Chris) and being able to speak up and communicate with an English-speaking boss (Chris), customers (Eva) and a salesperson at a mall (Irma).

Dynamic job needs: Apply-work-promotion-avoid exploitation

In addition to superación, the data revealed that the participants seemed to want to invest in learning English for their dynamic job needs, including applying, working, being promoted and avoiding exploitation. This finding seems to add another facet of adult ELs' desires about job needs, because this study's finding gives richness to what job needs specifically refer to in an adult EL setting. In other words, job needs not only refers to being able to work, but also that adult ELs in this particular context view job needs from multiple and deeper perspectives.

Job application

For example, Domingo said that English writing and speaking are really important to him. When I asked what makes him think so, Domingo recounted that he wants to learn how to write and speak English because he wants to write applications for jobs and more opportunities:

Domingo: Well, I never go to a school or speak English. But, you know, it's a good idea for me to speak more better English or communicate for the other people. And, we need to start how to write and read because I speak English but no, no idea how to write it, all the letters together. You know? Because it's really important, read and writing and speak.

I: Okay.

Domingo: Yeah.

I: So, you said you want to speak better. But also you want to write and read better, because reading and writing is important?

Domingo: Right.

I: So, in your life, why do you think speaking is important, writing and reading is important?

Domingo: Because you have more opportunity and when you go in the office and really want paper on something. When you, put application in the companies. When you no writing, and have no idea how to write, we need help from somebody else. That's why, you know, we need somebody else, helping you. And when you do writing or reading, you know how to make application or writing application. Yeah.

Work

In addition to job applications, English seems necessary for all participants at their place of work and in performing their duties. For Eva and Elsa, all customers to their restaurant are English speakers, so they need to learn English. As Elsa specifically works as a waitress, she feels this need directly:

I go to start [practicing English] more in the restaurant, because I see White people, more the customers is White people and talk English, English, English. And I need practice my English.

For Chris' job needs, he seems to want to work better by communicating effectively with job-related people. For example, when he goes to the hardware store each morning to buy construction materials such as lumber, he needs English. When he visits a work site, it is usually an

English-speaking customer's house. Chris feels that he wants to invest more in learning English:

> Because in my job, I have to know [English] because I have to go to a store and get stuff [lumber] for work and the stores it's like only English. ... When I wake up my cousin [boss] told me 'you have to learn [English] somewhere' and the job is like this. When I go to house [of a client], I have to ask you [the client] 'what do you want [me] to do right here?' I go to different jobs when like today I go to a house for doing a pool, concrete. Yeah, I have to ask something like, 'what do you need' and, yeah. I have to talk [English]

This work performance-related English need is also echoed in Mag's case. Mag recounted that she needs English to work with colleagues because she is currently the only Mexican at work. In the past, some colleagues spoke Spanish, but now her colleagues only speak English. At the same time, Mag seems to take this situation as a good opportunity for English practice:

> I just try to learn more because in my job I work a lot of times with, like people, they speak English and Spanish very good before. So sometimes is okay for me. But, if I don't speak very good English, because I have all the time translation. But now, in my job I am the only Mexican, so my boss she speak just English.

For daily work tasks, Domingo needs English to read the map of work orders. He said that he now understands all the vocabulary words on the map, words like kitchen, bedroom and yard. However, in the past he didn't know these words at all, so his boss read them and pointed out the map and the locations of a house one by one to him:

> Well, because we now, I build the house and we need understand the plan, the map. You know? It got letters and I don't know what that [the letters] say, the map and the plan. What is the labels, you know, like, how much is that, sometimes having numbers and sometimes having letters, and you know, like, I don't know what it says. What is the kitchen? Was there, the office? Yeah, my boss explained. Well, my boss is writing and then the flooring. He say 'the floor is right in, this is the office on the map. This is the kitchen. This is the bed'. Yeah. You stand there and know what he said right there. Sometimes. Right now, I understand the words kitchen, bed, but not before.

Promotion

After applying and working in a job for a certain amount of time, employees want promotion, as do the six participants. However, for their promotion opportunity, it seems that they must possess good English proficiency, which seems to lead them to invest in learning English. For example, Mag reported that she was offered a better position working in the office, as long as she had good English proficiency:

> I have opportunity in my job. My boss, he want me work in the office. But he ask, I need clear English, because I and I tried, I wanted [the promotion]. That, that is the reason I start to learn English. Because my boss tell me, 'I can give you job here in the office, but you need to learn English'.

Domingo also recounted that he needs more English and a GED degree to be promoted to a better position – working inside. To him, working outside is hard, tiring and heavy (see Figure 6.1). He wants to work inside. He knows that he needs more English and a GED for that, so he wanted to invest to learn English:

> Because, well, right now I'm working outside in the construction. Maybe with my GED, I work in a store or an office maybe. You know, like different... Why? Because I think inside is more better. You know, like when the air is more like cold, inside is not hot, and you know, more relaxed. You know...outside is... Hot. Sweat. Tired, and more heavy.

Figure 6.1 Domingo's outside workplace – he describes working outside as hard, sweaty and tiring. Domingo wants to work inside, which made him invest in learning English

Avoid exploitation

Lastly, investing to learn English to avoid job exploitation was reported. The participants said that sometimes their bosses order them to do difficult things. For example, Irma recalled that when her English was not proficient enough, her boss asked her to carry a heavy box. Irma told her boss that she could not carry it, but there was no clear communication. Irma was forced to carry the heavy box, which was hard for her:

Irma: More jobs. No, heavy.
I: Heavy?
Irma: Heavy.
I: Okay.
Irma: Because I think when we no speak English, they give the jobs more heavy.
I: Oh, really?
Irma: Yeah.
I: Ah, for example? Can you give me an example?
Irma: For example, um, in my other job, they told me to pick up heavy box, deep box.
I: Heavy box.
Irma: Uh-huh [Yes] and he said, 'go and pick it up Irma', and I say [not clearly] 'it's too heavy for me somebody can help', [and he said] 'no you can do it, you can do it for yourself'.
I: And at the time you didn't speak English much.
Irma: Yeah. No. Not too much.

After carrying the heavy box, Irma saw a group of workers who could speak good English. They gave their opinions about carrying the box. The other people were then given 'lighter' work such as working on computers or paper cutting. To Irma this was not fair, because the workers are paid the same money regardless of whether they carry heavy boxes or cut paper. The only difference was how well you could speak your opinions in English. This incident seems to act as another driving force for Irma's decisions to invest in learning English:

Irma: [When Irma carries the heavy box] And the other people speak English, they say, 'No I don't want to, somebody can do that, not me'. And they [boss] go for other people, and the other people don't, can't say nothing have to do.
I: Just go pick up.
Irma: Yeah.
I: But someone who can speak English,
Irma: Yeah and when the other people, speak English more better, they put do something else.

I: Like, for example?
Irma: Like, go see that computer, go see that,
I: Paper.
Irma: The papers, yeah. Cut paper.
I: Easy job.
Irma: Yeah.
I: Same money?
Irma: Yeah, same money. It's not fair... yeah, not fair.

Mag's story about being offered a position working inside, which was given to someone else who spoke better English than Mag, seems to be somewhat consistent with this finding – they need English to avoid work exploitation. Mag's job was working outside on a drawer assembly line, using a nail gun, with wood powders in the air causing many health risks. Mag wanted to go inside, just like Irma who didn't want to carry the heavy box, but both were not equipped with enough English proficiency, so they remained in the same undesirable situations – using a nail gun for Mag and carrying a heavy box for Irma.

Scholars have quantitatively investigated the job needs of adult EL populations (Valentine, 1990). Detailed, rich stories and narratives of job needs for this population have also been conducted. In their qualitative research, Derwing (2003), Han (2009) and Hyman (2002) reported the job needs for being able to work at sites, the second subcategory of this study's dynamic job needs finding. However, few studies have explored the other facets of job needs, such as being able to write application forms (Domingo) and avoiding job exploitation for heavy and risky work (Irma, Mag). This finding seems to fill the gap by letting adult ELs' untold voices be heard in rich and vigorous narratives.

Desire to communicate

The data revealed that another strong factor for the participants' decision to invest in English learning is that they have a desire to communicate with others. In fact, this seems to work as a means of supporting their aforementioned reasons, such as superación and dynamic job needs. For example, Mag said that she wants to communicate with people in stores, schools and hospitals by improving her English. Although translation is sometimes available, Mag has a strong desire to talk to people directly:

> I would like to communicate with the people, at the stores and they at school, the doctor. At appointment, the doctor he not speak Spanish, I don't understand. When I have appointments when I go to the doctor. I don't understand what they say. Yeah some is hard when you go to the stores or like doctors or you try to get some papers for the kids and you don't speak English. You feel like embarrassed...On the school day

[teacher-parent conference day] some people speak Spanish, they have translators, but it is better for me if I can understand to the teacher [directly].

Domingo also reported that he wants to learn English to communicate with people at his work. Domingo recently started translating between his boss and colleagues using English and Spanish:

I: And communicate also means with your boss?

Domingo: Well, yeah, with my boss. With the other people working with him.

I: And in your company?

Domingo: And in the company.

I: Do you have any example?

Domingo: Example, when, my boss say. My worker people say, 'what did boss say?' You know, they no idea. The boss talking to you. But I don't know how you speak to other.

I: How you explain...

Domingo: How you explain with other, what he said was.

I: So, when your boss told you something, you want to explain it to your, other people working together.

Domingo: To the other people. Yeah.

I: Other workers.

Domingo: Mhmm.

I: But you said you didn't know how to do that. You remember an example?

Domingo: Example. We'll say. And work in the garage. Boss say, 'the garage, working over there, to do, finish or something and like in the garage or in the kitchen'. I tell other working people, I say go and finish the kitchen. So I say.

In addition to his desire to talk with people at work, Domingo also pointed out that he wants to communicate with his neighbor:

You know, like, talking with your neighbors. Not like with him. You need to see who is your neighbor. Is good person, bad person, you know, like, what he's doing. I think it's really important.

Another layer of the desire to communicate was the need to communicate with their family members. Chris recounted that he wants to invest in learning English to communicate with his nephews who were born in the US:

Chris: I always talk with my nephews in English.

I: In Mexico?

Chris: No right here.
I: Your nephew?
Chris: Yes, I have nephews right here.

Chris' sister who lives in the US, his nephews' mother, has limited English proficiency. Chris wants to teach her English by taking English classes. He pointed out that teaching his family English is his sixth reason for investing in learning English:

Chris: Six, family [sixth reason to learn English]. Because my family, she don't speak English.
I: Your sister?
Chris: No English. My sister she don't know English.
I: Family, you said you want to teach English to your...
Chris: My sister.

Chris' twin sister who lives in Mexico once said to Chris that she wants to come to the US someday. Chris seems to want to teach his twin sister English too:

I: Ah good, good. Alright so okay, maybe you said you want to bring your sister here?
Chris: Sometimes yeah. I will bring her. I asked her.
I: Her. And she said what?
Chris: Yes, she said yes. I want to teach my sister English.

Desire to communicate with medical doctors was thematically reported across all six participants: for medical issues with her son's ears (Mag); when his son hit a door and injured his forehead (Domingo); when her husband passed away (Irma); when her sister had a stomachache (Elsa); when her daughter was sick (Eva); and when his friend was injured while playing football (Chris).

The data shows that the desire to communicate is used as a means of achieving superación and dynamic job needs. For example, Domingo's superación – being able to read and speak English for his children's education and future opportunities – can be achieved through improving his communicating capabilities (desire to communicate), which in turn can be used to achieve his other goal, to better communicate at his work (job: work). The detailed characteristics and colors of this finding of desire to communicate seem to be based on the study participants' unique contexts, where they are physical laborers, full-time workers and parents, who support family both in Mexico and in the US, and have a strong desire for superación for their own idiosyncratic situatedness.

Theme 6: Hardships – Different Priorities – Essentiality – More Opportunities

In addition to the three categories in Theme 5, all the participants seemed to have experienced hardship due to low English proficiency, which seems to give them the feeling that English is essential to live in the US. At the same time, all the participants have different priorities for why they want to learn English. Also, it seems that learning English means more opportunities for themselves and their family. All seven aspects of Themes 5 and 6 in a dynamic cluster seem to influence the participants to invest in their English learning.

Hardships due to low English proficiency

As discussed in Chapter 5, the participants experienced language barriers in their lives. Along with these language barriers, the data revealed that the participants underwent hardships due to low English proficiency, which seems to be another factor in their decision to invest in English learning. Irma experienced hardship when her previous husband was sent to an emergency room. She couldn't do anything and had her daughters translate their father's death. Mag experienced a similar hardship of not understanding the doctors' explanations about her son's ear problems. For Elsa, her daughter was sick and unable to translate, which was another hardship for Elsa. Domingo had similar hardship experiences when his son had a hernia. The doctor and nurse didn't explain verbally and just gave him papers to read:

Domingo: Well, right now, but, for my kids, hernia.
I: For his body?
Domingo: Yeah. And when take to the doctor. Like what happened with the kid you know, when it was the paper. And sometimes got in trouble because I don't know what the paper say. How, what happened with it, with the paper. You know, a bunch of time, questions asking what happened.
I: Yeah.
Domingo: And the doctor or the nurse only give me the paper. But I don't want to see the paper, but talk to understand.

These hardships were reported multiple times, and the meaning of each experience varied with each individual. However, one thematic pattern that emerged out of these hardship experiences is that it seems to work as a motivational factor for the adult ELs to keep investing in learning English. The following narratives seem to show the probable connections between their hardship experiences and their desire to invest in English learning:

I don't know what the [medical] paper say... we need to start, how to write and read because I speak English but no, no idea how read and write it... all the letters together. You know? Because it's really important, really important, read and writing and speak. (Domingo)

At appointment, the doctor, I don't understand... I always want to learn English. (Mag)

'Cause I need to learn English, I mean. For everything. (Eva)

I come because I want to learn English. (Chris)

Yeah, I interest going back to school, to learn English. I want better life, and protect my children. (Irma)

When my daught was sick, I went to emergency room, I can't speak English because my English was gone... I go to my English class. 'Cause I want to learn. (Elsa)

Different priorities

All six participants reported different priorities for what makes them decide to invest in learning English. The top four overarching reasons reported include (1) superación, (2) job, (3) communicate and (4) hospital. Aside from the thematic overarching priorities that emerged through all six participants, several unique priorities were also reported, such as buying products at stores, living in the US, helping other people and wanting to teach family members English.

One interesting phenomenon was that half the participants changed the ranking of their priorities after thinking about it for approximately 10 minutes. The question they were asked was 'Why do you want to learn English? Please make a list and prioritize based on the importance'. During the interviews, I helped the participants brainstorm for ideas. Most of the participants told me and wrote down life-related needs first, such as job, hospital and stores. But when I explained about a blank field where they could write down their own priority, the participants thought about it, wrote a word and put the new word at the top of the list. The word was superación. For example, at first Mag wrote down (1) job, (2) school (children) and (3) doctors. However, when she realized that there was room (blank spot) to write her opinion, she put superación in that spot and put it at the top of the list. Her list became (1) superación, (2) job, (3) school (children), (4) doctors and (5) store (Figure 6.2).

This 'priority rank changing' phenomenon also occurred with Domingo and Irma. Throughout the interviews, they seemed to think about the list and change it by putting the superación aspect at the top. Domingo first put job as his number one priority. Then, he changed the order by putting 'hope for kids as his superación' as his new priority. Likewise, Irma initially put job as her number one reason, but changed it

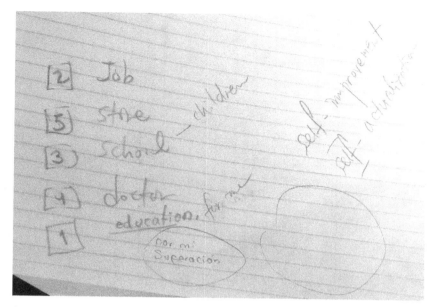

Figure 6.2 Priority list for Mag – she changed her choices by creatively writing 'super-ación' on the bottom and changing the ranks to make superación #1

to 'protecting my kids as superación' as her top priority. The other three participants, Eva, Elsa and Chris, first put superación for their number one reason. Table 6.1 illustrates each participant's different priorities for why they want to invest in learning English.

Each individual has different priorities for why they want to invest in learning English. It seems that their unique backgrounds may have impacted this decision. It is worth noting that this priority is not static, but dynamically changes its shapes and characteristics according to life situations. For example, when Eva's daughter Delma was young, helping Delma was her first reason for learning English, as reflected in the phrase 'School (kids)' in Eva's column in Table 6.1. However, Eva recounted that now that Delma is grown up, it might be her turn to pursue her own superación by putting it as number one and putting school (kids) as number three:

> Okay, maybe, in the long time before, when Delma was little, maybe my priority was Delma and Delma school. Maybe now she is big, grow up, she go to college. Okay it is my time.

Domingo also said that giving hope to his children by learning English, a unique form of superación to Domingo, takes first priority at this time. Although Domingo seems to have a desire to improve his English for his job and his own development (earning a GED degree), he said that

Table 6.1 Individuals' different priorities for why they want to invest in learning English

Priority	Mag	Domingo	Irma	Eva	Elsa	Chris
#1	Superación (better person)	Superación (hope for kids)	Superación (protecting kids)	Superación (fast speaking and listen)	Superación (self-education, college)	Superación (self-education)
#2	Job (promotion)	Communicate in job (boss, colleagues)	Communicate in job	Work	School (teacher–parent conference)	Job (buying materials)
#3	School (kids)	Hospital (kid's hernia)	Hospital (kids and me)	School (kids)	Communicate	Girlfriend
#4	Doctor (kid's ear tube)	GED (self-education)	Helping other people	Living in America	Doctor	Hospital
#5	Store		School	Doctor	Living in America	Communicate
#6			Shopping		Work	Teach family English

giving hope to his children by learning English is more important than anything else at this moment:

> For the child, I think this one, hope for my kids, is really important. Yeah. Because, you know, I am a dad and a supporter now. Because a child, this is more important... My kid is, like, right now it's more important. My hope to my kids is more important for me right now, more than my work and my GED.

Several deviant cases were also reported. Irma's fourth priority was 'helping other people' which was unique and not reported by others. In addition, Eva's eighth reason was 'opening more doors in the US' by learning English, which can be rephrased as 'more opportunities'. Lastly, Chris reported that he wants to learn English to teach his family, and for his two sisters – one in the US and the other in Mexico.

English is essential

Another thematic finding was that to the participants, learning English is essential for their lives in the US. This finding seems based on their immediate life needs such as grocery shopping, purchasing clothes and feeling comfortable in everything they do in an English-speaking country. For example, Chris reported that English is very important to him because he cannot live without it for his basic life needs, such as food and shoes. To him, English is a support:

Chris: English is like support, like support.
I: Support?
Chris: Because if you don't know English,
I: If you don't understand, uh huh.
Chris: If you don't know English, I live right here in the US I can't live like right here. I can't. Because as English is necessary, because when I go to a store and for example food.
I: For example food...
Chris: Food or shoes or things. Support.

For Eva, English is essential because she said everything outside her house is English. Eva pointed out that within her house, English is not needed, but outside, she needs it for everything. This seems to work as a factor in her decision to invest in English:

I: [You said] English for Eva, and you say everything-
Eva: Same. Yeah. For everything.
I: What do you mean by everything?
Eva: I mean everything. For the..., okay, maybe in my home, inside home, I don't need English. Outside I need English for everything.

Eva further emphasized the importance of English for out-of-house issues, by saying that she needs English for 'all problems in the world':

Yeah, cause I need to talk to teachers, the conference. Doctor appointments. Hospital. And then, and, all the problems in the world.

Elsa seems to expand Eva's thought by saying English is needed for living in the US. Elsa seems to disagree with the idea that 'you have to speak English because you live in the US', as her White co-workers claimed. Elsa heard this comment when she talked in Spanish with Eva at work. It seems that her White colleague didn't understand Elsa and Eva's Spanish conversation, so the colleague asked them to speak English with the rationale 'you speak English because you live in the US'. However, Elsa seems to critique this 'forceful' way of pushing her to learn English:

> And then other people say they live in America. Yeah, people don't like speak Spanish. Some people said, 'no. you speak English cause you live in America'. And I say 'I no'. But for me it's more easy speak Spanish. More easy and more fast, speak Spanish. I want speak English, but I can't. Because Eva and I were in the restaurant and the White guy, because Eva and I talk fast but more easy and more fast speak in Spanish. He was working in the kitchen, he didn't like we speak Spanish. He said 'you speak English because you live in America', I said, 'No, you need to speak Spanish', He said, 'English', and I said 'no you need to learn Spanish. No, 'cause I live in America. I can speak Spanish with my friend Eva'.

Elsa's rationale for saying 'no' to 'you speak English because you live in America' seemed to be based on her thought that she doesn't care if White people cannot speak Spanish when they visit Mexico:

> Yes, he's White guy. And he said, 'no you live in America, you need to speak English. Talk English'. And I say 'no you need to learn Spanish for us', and I said 'no, because I live in America. I don't care when you, people, when White people go to Mexico, in Mexico, you no speak Spanish'. Okay. I say 'Ah'. White people go to speak Spanish in Mexico, or speak English or Spanish. I'm okay.

Ironically, however, Elsa simultaneously, to some degree, agrees with the statement because she realizes the necessity of speaking English in her daily life:

> But I need English for living in the United State... Because I live in America and more people speak English. And I have problems when I want to talk to somebody. I need English.

As shown, it seems that to the participants, English is essential not only for their daily lives and basic needs such as shopping for daily commodities, but also for working with colleagues and diverse events they need to deal with outside their houses.

More opportunities

Lastly, one recurring category for why the participants want to invest in English learning is for more opportunities in their lives. More opportunities could mean more money (Chris), chances for promotion (Irma), better job conditions (Domingo, Mag) or more open doors in the US (Elsa and Eva). For example, Irma recounted that she wanted more opportunities through learning English which would enable her to be more comfortable performing her daily work tasks and allow for potential promotional opportunities:

> Oh, I want to learn more English and perfection my English, because I want more opportunities, better opportunities. Because I feel more comfortable, more happy when with everybody. Because when I start one job, I see the difference when they come back. When somebody came and talk English, I think and I see better opportunities and better job. More better opportunities.

For Elsa, learning English means opening more doors, not only for herself but also for her children. It seems to work as another factor for her to invest in English learning:

> English open many doors. Like I said for work or everything, education... opportunities and everything. And because some people don't like speak Spanish and I want to speak very good English but I can't. I want English.

Chris recounted that if he spoke better English, he would make more money: '[I want to learn English] ... For more money and, opportunity yeah'.

The more opportunities category was reported in Chapter 5 as the participants' initial motivational factor to decide to come to the US from Mexico. It seems that this factor continually affects their ongoing decision criteria, based on their daily life experiences. In other words, the adult ELs seem to keep seeing the link between better English skills and better opportunities in the form of either monetary compensation, job promotions or educational opportunities. It seems that the concept of 'more opportunities' has been active in their decision-making processes from 13 or more years ago when they initially decided to come to the US.

Mapping Out of Investment Factors

To thematically map out what makes the participants decide to invest in learning English, I found probable patterns and themes over the seven categories: superación, dynamic job needs: apply-work-promotion-avoid exploitation, desire to communicate, hardships due to low English proficiency, different priorities, English is essential and more opportunities. It seems that the seven categories are interwoven and dynamically influence the adult ELs' decisions to invest in English learning.

First, it seems that the concept of superación embraces other factors in terms of what leads to the participants' decisions, such as dynamic job needs: apply-work-promotion-avoid exploitation, desire to communicate and more opportunities. This is because the data showed that the 'shapes and colors' or characteristics of superación (i.e. becoming a better person) are different for different individuals. Perhaps more importantly, the definition changes for the participants based on the time and situation that was encountered. For example, for Mag, moving forward to the next level in her job and improving her communication skills mean superación. For Eva, being able to quickly speak and listen is a facet of her superación. For Chris, being able to communicate with store workers and his boss for his job is an aspect of his superación. These examples show the probable link between superación and job categories. In addition, for Irma, her top superación aspect is to protect her children by being able to communicate in English. Irma's second superación aspect is to be able to actively communicate with other speakers of English and not say 'never mind', which seems to point more toward her individual development. Likewise, Eva's first superación aspect is not to remain silent. She doesn't want to say, 'Okay, I busy, bye', but rather, she wants to 'fast' talk and listen. These examples show the probable relation between superación and the desire to communicate. Lastly, Domingo's one aspect of superación is to be able to read English books for his children. This is more toward giving hope to his children and better opportunities for himself. For Elsa, going to college is an aspect of superación, which can converge with the concept of more opportunities. This last example shows the probable link between superación and more opportunities.

In addition to the intertwined relationships between these four categories, the other three categories also seem to dynamically relate to each other (hardship due to low English proficiency, English is essential, different priorities). For example, Irma's hardship experience, when she remained silent on the day her husband passed away, seems to influence her to think that learning English is essential in the US, which in turn seems to affect the priority of her English learning.

Furthermore, the three categories (hardship due to low English proficiency, English is essential, different priorities) seem to be related to the aforementioned four categories in the participants' final decision to invest in learning English. For example, the participants' hardship experiences, e.g. Mag's experiences of being silent at a doctor's appointment for her son's ears seems to lead to her desire to communicate with doctors. This feeling of a desire to communicate also seems to relate with Mag's job needs and feelings about more opportunities through learning English (recall that Mag was offered a promotion to work inside, as long as her English was good enough). This more opportunities feeling seems to influence her list of different priorities at that time, as Mag put 'job' as her second priority for why she wants to learn English following her number one reason – superación.

Characteristics of Investment Factors:
Alive and Dynamically Moving

All in all, these seven categories (superación, dynamic job needs: apply-work-promotion-avoid exploitation, desire to communicate, hardships due to low English proficiency, different priorities, English is essential and more opportunities) for what makes adult ELs at the CEL invest in English learning seem to dynamically work together in participants' final decisions to learn English. Although I found that each category is probably weighted differently, the more important finding seems to be that these categories are not static, but rather are alive and dynamically moving based on the time and situation that the individuals encounter. For example, Eva previously said that supporting Delma was her top priority and was equal to her superación at that time. However, Eva points out that now learning English is maybe for her own development. She infers that she puts her own self-improvement as her top priority, as a current form of her superación, by putting Delma as the second priority – because Delma is now grown up and a college student. This finding seems consistent with previous research that points to the importance of the situatedness of individual students in their learning (Gee, 2012, 2014; Lave & Wenger, 1991). It seems worthwhile to note that the driving factors for adult ELs' investment in English learning are strongly and complicatedly connected to their situatedness, which is diverse and ever-changing over time.

Figure 6.3 illustrates the probable thematic links across Research Question 2 findings about what drives adult ELs to invest in learning English. The dotted-line square with the title superación embraces the three sub-squares of dynamic job needs: apply-work-promotion-avoid exploitation, desire to communicate and more opportunities. The bidirectional arrows among them show the intertwined relationships among the three. On the bottom of the diagram are three categories interacting with each other as other underlying facets of what makes the participants invest in learning English, including hardships due to low English proficiency, English is essential and different priorities. The arrows among them show their probable interrelatedness, and the dotted box surrounding those three categories shows the probable cluster of the three

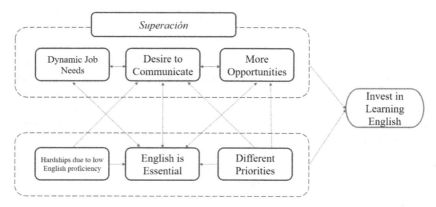

Figure 6.3 Map of investment factors – the seven categories seem related to each other in an intertwined way, which seems to dynamically influence the adult ELs' decisions to invest in English learning

categories compared to the above three categories under superación. The arrows across the two dotted-line clusters on the top and bottom show the dynamic and subtle relationships among all seven categories. On the right side of the diagram, the two arrows converging to the terminal decision titled 'Invest in Learning English' show the probable causal relationships between the seven categories as a complex and holistic factor, and the participants' final decision to invest.

Holistic Mapping between 'Who They Are' and Investment Factors

While thematically mapping the findings of the investment factors, I found that the diverse aspects of who the adult ELs are, discussed in Chapter 5, seem to foreground the investment factor findings. It would be foundational to recount the foregrounding aspects: the linkages connected across the three categories in who the adult ELs are living in the US for 13+ years, language barriers at work, family and community, and the desire to learn English. Specifically, the category desire to learn English reported in Chapter 5 seems to be expanded through the investment factor findings. Just as we can enlarge a smartphone app icon on our phone screen to reveal a larger activation mode when we touch it, it seems that the desire to learn English category reported in Chapter 5 can be expanded to the seven categories of investment factors. Figure 6.4 illustrates this probable intertwined relationship.

Discussion of What Drives Investment through Theorizing

The seven reasons for investing that the adult ELs pointed out seem to be consistent with Darvin and Norton's (2015) notions of capital in their investment framework: economic capital, cultural capital and social

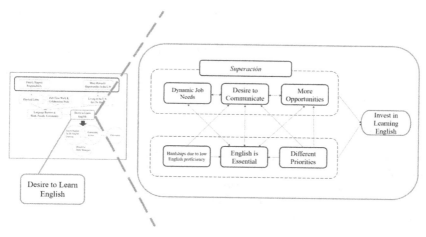

Figure 6.4 A probable intertwined relationship between who they are and investment factors – it seems that the category 'desire to learn English' foregrounds the investment factors and is then expanded

capital. In their investment framework, Darvin and Norton (2015) view that L2 learners invest based on the intertwined influence of their diverse needs, positioning rationale and decisions based on their ideology, identity and capital. Specifically for capital, they used Bourdieu's (1987) view to specify three notions: economic capital (wealth, property, income), cultural capital (knowledge, educational credentials) and social capital (connections to networks of power). In this study's case, the participants' reasons for investing in English seem to be consistent with these three components of capital. For example, the participants reported economic capital to gain through learning English, such as food and shoes (Chris), cars and houses (Mag, Elsa, Irma) and money (Domingo, Chris). As a form of cultural capital, all participants reported their educational development needs. Lastly, for social capital, learning English to ask for help seems consistent with that notion, such as seeking help for medical situations (Irma, Mag, Domingo, Elsa, Eva, Chris) and wanting to communicate with colleagues and customers (Eva, Elsa).

In addition, the desire to communicate category seems to be consistent with Darvin and Norton's (2015) identity notion, which emphasized that individual learners consistently negotiate and position their spaces with other conversation interlocutors within evolving power structures. For example, Irma, Chris and Domingo's examples of staying silent when English-speaking situations overwhelmed them seem to share the notions of identity struggle and refusing power. They seem to refuse their power to speak out because they feel that their English is not legitimate enough to be included in the communication situation. However, it is worthwhile noting that participants' identities in the communication site and their positioning are ever-evolving and changing in order to speak up about their rights, such as asking their colleagues to learn Spanish to communicate with them (Eva, Elsa), asking clarification from his girlfriend (Chris) and asking clarification from her boss by saying 'excuse me, I don't understand, could you please tell me one more time?' (Irma). For EL educators, understanding this identity negotiation based on the power structure and hegemonic aspects (where students might feel that they are not legitimate enough to join in fast-paced and fluent English-speaking contexts) is important, because EL learners by nature keep negotiating their identities and positions to assess whether or not they can be included or excluded.

To connect to the capital notion, when refusing their power to speak or being excluded, their potential capital for economic, social and cultural gains through English seems to disappear. It seems that although the participants in this study had a high desire to invest initially, at the same time, they keep assessing, questioning and navigating their identity, right to speak and whether or not taking this class is beneficial for their capital building.

Throughout Chapter 6, I found that what drives adult ELs to invest in learning English is based on their superación as well as real-life hardships, needs and priorities, which are all mixed together. Although it was the case that all six participants decided to invest, it turned out that five of them dropped out physically at a point in their English learning journey at the CEL. While Chris was physically present in his EL classes, more narrative data showed that his mind was absent. Chapter 7 explores what makes the adult ELs at the CEL drop out or stay in their English class.

7 What Makes Adult ELs Drop Out

For context, it is essential to note that there were three teachers in this book's study: teacher John, teacher Amy and teacher Derek (pseudonyms). Table 7.1 illustrates when each individual dropped out. 'Stay' means that the participants stayed with the teachers written on the far-left column. 'Drop' means that the participants dropped out while taking classes with that teacher. Elsa in the middle has both stay and drop, which means that Elsa took one class with the teacher and after that she dropped out. This chapter will address diverse dropout factors and the holistic and thematic map among the factors to explore what makes adult English learners (ELs) drop out.

Ten categories were reported as dropout factors: learn nothing, teacher apathy, feeling oppressed, waste of time, just talk-talk-talk, no prep, boring, unrelated topics, unmet expectations and different perspectives and reactions. Of these 10 categories, four themes emerged thematically. Theme by theme, this chapter addresses what made participants decide to drop out.

Table 7.1 When the participants dropped out

	Mag	Eva	Elsa	Irma	Domingo	Chris
Teacher John class	Stay	Stay	Stay	Stay	Stay	Stay
Teacher Derek class	Stay	Stay	Stay/drop	Drop	Stay	Stay
Teacher Amy class	Drop	Drop	Drop	Drop	Drop	Stay

Note: Teachers' and students' names are pseudonyms.

Theme 7: Learn Nothing – Teacher Apathy – Feeling Oppressed: Waste of Time

Learn Nothing

The data revealed that adult ELs at the Center for English Literacy (CEL) seem to drop out because they learned nothing, had teacher apathy and felt oppressed, which simultaneously and eventually seemed to make them feel that the class was a waste of time. For example, Mag, in teacher Amy's class, seemed to feel that she learned nothing from the teacher and that the teacher just talked to other classmates, regardless of whether Mag understood the class topic under discussion. This incident also simultaneously seemed to give Mag the feelings of not being cared about and feelings of oppression:

Mag: With teacher Amy, she just speak with people [who] understand [English better], she just speak. Amy she just speak. She just speak with the people like they speak more English.

I: Students like your husband [who speaks better English] maybe?

Mag: Yeah, like and like him, Amy don't worry about me. So teacher just speak what, what thing you say.

I: For example, Amy just talk to...

Mag: Yeah it is like, we just talk about. You just tried to teach me because I understand a little bit. And she understands, so she don't teach nothing [anything] to me.

This type of incident with feelings of learning nothing and that the teacher only talked to other students who spoke better English, seemed to eventually make Mag think that the class is a waste of time:

> I feel like learn nothing. I feel she don't care me learning. No, like I don't learn nothing, I don't learn nothing. Oh is like, she, teacher is wasted time.

This learn nothing feeling was shared with Irma while she took teacher Derek's class, which seemed to trigger Irma to drop out. Irma recalled that one night, she felt that Derek was not prepared for the class and that she had learned nothing, which eventually seemed to lead Irma to the decision, 'me no more come':

Irma: Yeah. No more come.

I: Okay and can you tell me why? What makes you say, okay I don't want to come?

Irma: That one, that reason because he no same, no chose same like other teacher.

I: For example?

Irma: For example, no make that little groups. Don't bring. Nothing prepared and he asks about movies. Things about no meaning, nothing. And, what else, when I see in my notes [using my classes], my journal. When I see nothing [in my notes; Irma checked her notes for Derek's classes, there were no notes left], it mean there is none.

I: In teacher Derek's class?

Irma: Uh-huh. I say no, no come more.
I: You learned nothing.
Irma: Uh-huh.

Irma also recounted that the connection between feelings of learning nothing – don't want to come anymore were shared with other class-mates over break time. She recalled that one night, Eva, Mag and Irma talked and shared feelings about learning nothing and waste of time:

> When we are in the break time and when we go home outside, Eva, she said, 'oh maybe I don't come back, no came more because the teacher, I no like it' And I say 'why', she [Eva] said 'because the teacher is not learn like teacher John'. 'When John is coming?' and I say, well pastor say 'two weeks'. Two weeks that John not here. Oh, okay, maybe 'we back when John back' I say', yeah I think me too'. And she [Eva] said, 'yeah because he's, I, no learn nothing. It's only waste time'. Eva and Mag, too. Yeah, because she [Mag] want learn English. She want English. Yeah, they want, Eva and Mag, she want to learn English.

Domingo also reported this feeling of learning nothing or, in his own words, learning no 'information'. To Domingo, '(correct) infor-mation' to correct his English knowledge or learning new 'informa-tion' seemed to mean learning something new. Domingo said that, even though he was tired, he comes to English class to learn new infor-mation because the new information is good for his mind, not for his body. He recounted that he didn't learn any 'information' in teacher Amy's class:

Domingo: Now, what's great, oh okay, I got it, the new *information*, you know, it's not great all the time, you know? It's why I come, you know like when it's time for something new or speak cor-rect, important, right?
I: So, even though you are tired you come because you learn new and correct information?
Domingo: New information, correct information.
I: For your mind,
Domingo: Mhmm, for mind.
I: Not for your body,
Domingo: Not for body. Yeah.
I: Okay, okay. Your body's tired but you come.
Domingo: Yes. But, teacher Amy class. Not very information. No information.

For Chris, although he wanted to ask his teachers to explain and repeat what they said when he didn't understand, it seems that the teachers didn't explain again. These incidents seemed to make Chris feel that he didn't understand, with the consequent feelings of embarrassment and of learning nothing:

I: What about Derek's class you understand everything for that?
Chris: No. Because it was like, I get embarrassed with him and I don't know.
I: You said he speak too fast or?
Chris: Yeah, too fast. And he [Derek] not repeat,
I: And he didn't repeat it, just keep saying...
Chris: Yeah. And then Derek he was like, him right there, [staying] quiet.

It seems that teacher Derek was quiet and provided no further explanations, which seemed to make Chris feel that the lesson was boring and he didn't learn anything from it. The concept of 'boring' will be discussed separately in the following themes. However, it seems worthwhile to briefly address the boring-ness here, because, to Eva and Elsa, teacher Amy's class was not boring, but it seemed that they learned nothing from her class:

Eva: She's [Amy] funny, funny but no learning.
I: Okay.
Elsa: But no learning,
Eva: For the class, no learning, no, laugh too much.
I: No learning?
Elsa: Not too much.
I: Okay.
Elsa: Is fun, is funny.
I: But you don't learn?
Eva: She is good, but no more learning.

Teacher apathy

It seems that the feeling of learning nothing simultaneously triggered two categories, feeling not cared about (teacher apathy) and feeling oppressed, and these three categories seemed to eventually lead the participants to decide to drop out. For example, Chris reported that Amy didn't care whether Chris understood the learning content, providing him with no further explanation, which led him to think that the teacher didn't care about him:

Chris: If it, I don't understand when teacher Amy, like she don't like care.

Amy didn't... explain... No Explain.

Irma also had the feeling of not being cared about by her teachers. She recounted that other teachers seemed to have no interest in or didn't care about helping her improve her English:

> And my other teachers, I think he can or they show, or learn, no very good interest [in us]. No, no, it's like no good. Well, if I think they say, well if she or he learn, it's okay, if no learn, the teacher looks saying, 'I don't care'. Yeah, maybe teacher don't care if we learn or not.

Eva and Elsa recounted that teachers Amy and Derek seemed not to care about them as well, because they said they could see the teachers' attitude. Although Eva and Elsa asked about their linguistic mistakes and how to correct them, all they heard was 'it's not important', which seemed to give them the feeling of not being cared about:

I: What about language mistakes, you make mistakes right in class? So, I think mistake is good but did the other teacher say anything about your mistake?
Eva: Uh-huh. They said it's not important.
I: It's not important? Really.
Elsa: They said for me. I don't know that many people.
I: Do you remember an example you ask a question and they say it's not important?
Eva: No.
Elsa: No, no say this word but you can see the attitude.

For Domingo, feelings of not being cared about and of being oppressed/ignored recurred through many incidents in addition to when he heard 'quiet' while he translated for his classmates. It seems that Domingo felt that he was not being cared about when his teachers didn't give him enough time to 'copy (write down)' the words and sentences the teacher had written on the whiteboard. He recounted that giving him no time and just erasing the words was wrong, because it seemed to take away his learning opportunities, while simultaneously promoting feelings of not being cared about and ignored:

Domingo: Yeah, but it's [copying whiteboard writing to notebooks] no, no, not simple. Something, you know, copy writings faster is important. It's when, it's, when start this example and when finished. Teacher erase it.
I: They erase it?
Domingo: Erase it.
I: Ah.

Domingo: And then, I, I had a hard time but, you know, like copy that…
          Right? Because I don't know, don't have time for.
I: So, no time to practice?
Domingo: No time for copy and practice.
I: They just write and-
Domingo: Yeah.
I: I see…
Domingo: And [teachers said] go, and go.
I: Okay. What do you think about that? How do you feel about
          it?
Domingo: I think it's wrong.

Feeling oppressed

Along with the feeling of not being cared about, feeling oppressed
also emerged as a dropout factor. It seems that feeling oppressed derived
from both learning nothing and teacher apathy. For Domingo, he felt
strongly oppressed when he heard teacher Amy call Chris 'stupid' one
night after Chris had asked a question. In fact, that night was Domingo's
last class. Domingo recounted that he cannot go to a teacher who calls
a student 'stupid', so he made his final decision to drop out that night:

Domingo: And then Chris said right there, calling… stupid.
I: What? Teacher Amy said to-
Domingo: To Chris.
I: To Chris? 'You are stupid?'
Domingo: You are stupid.
I: Why?
Domingo: I don't know. I don't know what he's asking, but 'Oh, no, you
          stupid'.
I: Ah. …but isn't that joking?
Domingo: No, not joking.
I: It was serious?
Domingo: Yeah, serious.
I: Ah.
Domingo: And then, so the other people, you know, like how you go to
          somebody else calling you stupid. Supposed to be, because I
          have to speak to other persons.
          …
Domingo: Yeah. Then, I don't come here, no more.

In addition, when they didn't understand, the participants wanted to
catch up by using an alternative approach, using their first language (L1) –
Spanish. For example, because Chris felt he was learning nothing and had
no understanding, he wanted to talk to his classmate (Domingo) using
Spanish to catch up on the class topics. 'Because if I don't understand

something I ask my friend in Spanish and he [Chris' friend] tell me in Spanish'. This help-seeking for better understanding using Spanish was shared with Mag too. Mag also asked Domingo to help her to comprehend what the teachers said using Spanish. But teacher Amy said 'quiet' when they used Spanish, which seemed to oppress the participants:

Domingo:	With Mag. We're talking one time and because you know, Mag is, say, 'no, no what?' You remember. Then, because she have no idea, Mag said, 'what do you say? No understand nothing. No'. [I said] 'Right now I think I understand a little bit'. But when Mag understand nothing. No. And one time, I was speaking with Mag [by translating into Spanish] and the teacher, Amy, said quiet.
I:	To teacher Amy?
Domingo:	No, Amy to me.
I:	Amy to you?
Domingo:	Amy said to me. No talking, quiet.

Likewise, for Chris, he also seemed to feel oppressed when his teachers didn't allow him to use Spanish. Chris understood and agreed with the policy of using English only, because it was an English class. However, when he didn't understand, he wanted to use Spanish for a moment, but Derek didn't allow it, which seemed to oppress him:

Chris:	No Spanish because I come in an English class but sometimes when I don't understand, I have to ask my friends in Spanish,
I:	You talk to your friends, right?
Chris:	My friends in Spanish. I talk to understand. Yeah.
I:	That was feeling good right. But teacher Derek said no?
Chris:	Derek said no, yeah.
I:	How do you feel about it?
Chris:	Not good, no good.

In addition to not being allowed to use their L1s in class, witnessing teachers only talking to a certain group of students who spoke better English seemed to oppress the participants. For example, Irma recalled that teacher Derek kept talking, although Irma didn't understand. Irma assumed that Derek thought her English as good as the other students to whom he talked:

Uh, no, I think Derek is, only he want talk like, like me no really English. He think maybe I know a lot of English like, talk and talk and talk. And he, no if me pronounce good or not good, he only talk and talk and talk. Maybe he, have another student learn more of me [who speaks English better than Irma], I guess is why he talk and talk and talk.

As reported earlier in this chapter, Mag recounted this feeling of oppression when her teachers only talked to other students who spoke better English. Interestingly, this oppressed feeling based on being in a similar situation – teachers ignoring them but talking to other students who spoke better English – was also reported by Eva and Elsa. Eva and Elsa experienced this type of oppression in the classes they had taken in the past. In Eva and Elsa's past experiences, other students even showed off their better English:

Elsa: Okay, in the long time in the past, I go all the class English and then, I don't like for them maybe too much people. And the one person maybe say 'oh, I have question'
Eva: Yes,
Elsa: [the other student said] 'Oh, I am more better than you and you'.
Elsa: [the other student said] 'I know more English than you'.
Eva: It's too much people. And then maybe, maybe me, I said okay I no talk, I no question,
I: Then you don't want to go maybe.
Elsa: Uh-huh, I no come back.

The teachers seemed to only talk to the students who showed off, giving Elsa and Eva no opportunities to talk or participate. This feeling of being ignored and oppressed from both peers and teachers made Elsa and Eva decide to drop out:

Elsa: ...some, some lady [who speaks better English] ask one question, the teacher go with her and no explain for everybody the question. No, go with her and explain personal and all the time is the same, in same class. Only, I say and I talk to the lady 'oh, and I say, I don't want anymore because all the time, same'.
I: So, they don't teach everyone but only one student.
Elsa: No, you, question with her. No explain this question for everybody learn. With her [the student], it's personal, teacher for her, I feel like, it waste my time.
Eva: Waste my time. And I say 'no, I don't want to come back next week' and she [Elsa] said, no me too—no come back no more. Sometimes cause the teacher.

An interesting point is that this is what happened to Eva and Elsa in the past, but not in this study. This time, they never reported this feeling of being oppressed/ignored due to being neglected by peers and teachers, but Irma, Mag and Chris did report such feelings in the current study. It seems that this time Eva and Elsa were in the 'conversation partner groups' and were regarded as speaking better English than Mag, Irma and other classmates. It seems that Eva and Elsa were unintentionally members of the oppressing group in the situation where Mag and Irma thought the teacher only talked to classmates with better English. It is worth recalling Mag's statement again, 'With teacher Amy she just speak with a people [who] understand [English better], she just speak... Amy she just speak... She just speak with the people like they speak more English'. Portraying the situation, when teacher Amy only talked to students who understood English better, those students seemed to include Eva and Elsa, but not Mag, Irma, Chris or others. Reflecting on Eva and Elsa's English proficiency when I taught and interviewed them, it seemed higher than their other classmates.

Waste of time

All in all, the feeling of learning nothing, not being cared about (teacher apathy) and feeling oppressed seemed to play a pivotal role in causing the participants to feel that the class was a waste of time, thus leading to the decision to drop out. Under the four dominant categories, six detailed intricacies were reported that seem to contribute each dominant factor. The next section will address the six subcategories regarding what made the participants drop out.

Theme 8: Just Talk, Talk, Talk – No Prep – Boring

The interview data revealed that the participants seemed to feel that the teachers just talk, talk, talk, which made them feel that the teachers made no preparations for the classes, thus they felt that the class was boring. This theme, in turn, seems to contribute to Theme 7 findings, the most dominant factor for dropping out: learning nothing, feeling not cared about (teacher apathy) and feeling oppressed.

Just talk, talk, talk

Mag recalled that teacher Amy just talked to students with good English, 'She just speak with the people like they speak more English'. Chris also recounted that teacher Amy spoke too fast, and just talked without interacting when his classmate Eva asked a question:

Chris: And I remember when Eva told her, teacher Amy, she speak fast.
I: So, teacher Amy speaks so fast.
Chris: So fast yeah. Just talk fast. She no care.

Domingo recounted that he didn't understand what the teacher was talking about because the teacher just talked, talked and talked:

Because, well, I think they, Amy, the teacher, does not have an idea or time for explanation and only talk, talk and talk so fast. That people is not understand what you're talking about. Right, and they, understand nothing that I'm leaving.

When I visited Irma and Domingo's Spanish congregation, Irma's husband Fernando (pseudonym) told me why students drop out. Fernando kept saying to me, 'the teacher just talk, talk, talk, no patience'. English teachers may believe that talking in the target language is authentic input, encouraging and positively challenging students to learn. However, the data in this study seems to show that just talk, talk, talk without communicating or caring decreases students' desire to invest and oppresses them, causing them to drop out.

No preparation

It seems that the students' perception of their teachers just talking made them think that the teachers were not prepared for class. For example, Irma recalled that Derek came to class and asked 'what the students want to learn', and suddenly suggested talking about movies. This incident made Irma feel that this teacher was not prepared:

> Um, two weeks, yeah for two weeks and he say that, 'tell me what do you want to learn?' I say, everybody say, 'I don't know' because we can't communicate with him and everybody only there... And he talking only about, the movies, 'what the, you see this movie?' Derek said, 'Do you see other movie, do you see um, what you think?' and I never see movies, in English, no English. No movie, no English movies, but, so I can't talk about that.

In general, talking about movies might be a good topic for ELs, but it was not a good, useful or shared topic for Irma. To Irma, this incident gave her the impression that teacher Derek had not prepared for the class, although Irma, as a student, had prepared for class. Irma thought this – teacher with no preparation – is probably why other classmates drop out:

Irma: Is why I think everybody no come anymore because he no, no bring like you. He don't bring nothing.
I: He bring nothing?
Irma: No, he bring like this and put right here but no got the program [class preparation]. No, nothing.
I: Okay, so he didn't prepare.
Irma: Uh-huh, no nothing. But, I, my friends prepare.
        Teacher just come. Only come. No prepare.

Irma recalled that, one night, teacher Derek forgot his journal and returned home to get it, which seemed to reinforce Irma's mindset about no preparation. All Irma remembers about what Derek did when he didn't prepare was talk, talk, talk:

Irma: And one day he say, 'oh man, I don't bring my journal, let me go'. And he go and he come back and 'oh no, sorry, sorry, I don't bring'.

I: Oh, okay, then what did you and teacher do?

Irma: Only talk, talk, talk.

For Eva and Elsa, the fact that the teacher didn't give a homework assignment, or didn't check homework assignments, or forgot about the homework meant that the teacher was not prepared. Elsa recalled that although she did her homework, teacher Amy forgot and didn't check the homework:

> Then teacher Amy maybe has homework but no check homework. Uh-huh no check. She forget. She no ask, no ask you bring in your homework or sometime they say yes, okay she no check.

Eva also reported that it seems that teacher Derek came to class without preparing. According to Eva, teacher Derek just came in and said okay and remained silent. Then, other classmates just talked in Spanish:

> Teacher Derek only, only come in and they say 'okay', one maybe only 2-3 English teaching, and the most time, people [classmates] talk everything, yeah, in Spanish. Only in Spanish. And the teacher only listen and they no understand. Yeah.

Here, it is worthwhile noting that at a certain point the participants started talking in Spanish, because the class was boring or a waste of time. Speaking in Spanish with classmates seems to make the time more meaningful to them. Basically, it seems that the participants didn't want to waste their time by listening to teachers who kept talking, didn't prepare and thus were boring:

> When you tell, no, when the class is no interesting or no learn, you don't care. You prefer, when the class is boring, I prefer to talk to Eva using Spanish. 'How are you today, what are things and week and all'.

Boring

Other participants acknowledged that not only did the teachers not prepare for class, but they also covered the same topic for several days running. For example, Eva and Elsa recalled that teacher Derek taught the same ABC alphabet class for three days, which bored the students:

Eva: Yeah, maybe they, in the Monday, maybe put two, three sentences, and the Wednesday, the same class, no different.

I: Oh, really.

Eva: Yeah.

I: For example, do you remember an example, the same sentence?

Elsa: Yeah, for a simple and then he has, for the letters who said okay, what is letters, A, next? B.

I: Yeah, the sound.

Elsa: Yeah. Maybe Monday and Wednesday and next Monday, same.

Eva: Yeah.

I: Oh, okay. Is that [the same ABC class for more days] what Derek did, Derek or Amy, maybe?

Eva: Derek. And, Derek is more boring.

Chris also recalled the days that teacher Derek continued to teach ABC letters. For Chris, it was also boring:

Chris: Yeah ABC always.

I: Always ABC. Oh really...

Chris: That's it.

I: How do you feel about that it's good or not good?

Chris: It's good but it was like boring.

Eva and Elsa recalled that teacher Amy used several game activities. Elsa said, 'Game is more better [not boring] her class, I think, is more better'. However, Mag took the game days as boring and not good for her learning, because it seems that teacher Amy played the same games for several days in a row, even though, according to Mag, the students seemed not to understand the games:

Mag: Amy, we play a lot of games

Mag: Wow. She [Amy] say you Mafia, you sheriff, you wake up! They more people, you know, mafia wake up!

Mag: I really don't understand it. Amy just want to know who want to eliminate the one.

I: Okay so you have no idea for the rule...

Mag: I think it was like this is okay but, not good for study.

I: How many games?

Mag: The mafia three times.

As for the Mafia game, Domingo also seemed to remain silent. It seems that the Mafia game was boring to Domingo:

Domingo: Yeah, the Mafia games, but only serious, no talking. Only quiet.

I: Quiet, oh really...

Domingo: Yeah.

I: You were silent.

Domingo: Yeah. Silent, and boring.

For Domingo, the teachers seemed unprepared when he saw them standing in the class and telling students what to do. For example, he recalled that teacher Amy didn't give any materials or examples, but just said 'make sentences' and waited silently, which made Domingo bored:

I: What about other teachers?
Domingo: Teacher only say 'make sentence'.
I: They didn't write an example on whiteboard?
Domingo: No. No example. Just say 'make sentence'. I boring.

It seems that the participants witnessed the teachers just talking, talking, talking with no class preparation, which made them feel that the class was boring. These three findings are closely related to other findings. The overarching relationships within a holistic context will be discussed with a diagram at the end of this chapter.

Theme 9: Unrelated Topics – Unmet Expectations

The participants also seemed to perceive that the class topics were unrelated to them, and the class activities didn't meet their expectations.

Unrelated topics

First, Irma's reactions to the topic of movies supported this finding as she said: 'I never see movies, in English, no English. No movie, no English movies but so I can't talk about that'. Mag, Eva and Elsa also recounted that the class was not interesting. For example, Elsa said she won't come anymore because 'No more interest the class'. Domingo also seemed to be frustrated when he didn't understand the topics that the teachers talked about: '...that people is not understand what you're [teacher's] talking about [topics]. Right, and they, understand [nothing] that I'm leaving'.

Unmet expectations

It seems that the students' expectations for learning methods and study strategies were not met. For example, Irma and Chris liked group work with their peers, but teachers Derek and Amy rarely did group work in the classes:

Yeah, yeah, no, and that teacher don't make groups like you, no. Only write and write, yeah. Sit down. Never say wake up. No groups. (Irma)

I like work in group, like with my friends and doing something and stand up, and read to other people. I like working in group... And everyone [other teachers] don't do that. (Chris)

Domingo and Mag expected to practice their English by repeating speeches and copying teachers' writings on the whiteboard. But the teachers seemed not to give such opportunities to them:

> I like Repeat, repeat, repeat. Practice, I like how you teach because you make questions and they [students] answer by, if they don't speak you'll repeat it again and we so practice. (Mag)

> I had a hard time but, you know, like copy the example. Right? Because I don't know, don't have time or. No time for copy and no time like practice. (Domingo)

This finding of unmet expectations is consistent with Gault (2003) and Han (2009) who found that a 'mismatch' between students' expectations and instructional practices work as a dropout factor.

Theme 10: Different Perspectives and Reactions

A final dropout factor, different perspectives and reactions to teachers' behaviors and input, emerged throughout the data. Some participants took the input to be more oppressive than others, which led them to drop out. However, other participants seemed not to take the same behaviors and inputs seriously. For example, the incident of hearing 'stupid' seemed to be interpreted in different ways among the participants. As reported earlier, this was a critical moment for Domingo's decision to drop out, because Domingo thought he couldn't go to a teacher who calls a student stupid. However, Eva and Elsa had different interpretations. According to Eva and Elsa, the situation when teacher Amy said 'stupid' to Chris was understandable. Eva and Elsa recounted that Chris asked Amy a stupid question about her boyfriend. To Eva and Elsa, the word 'stupid' derived from Chris' inappropriate question, thus Amy saying 'stupid' was not a serious problem to Eva and Elsa. After that incident, Eva and Elsa recalled that a man came to Amy's class and stayed:

Elsa: Stupid? Oh, because Chris sometime say...
I: You remember that?
Elsa: Yes, I remember um, it is because Chris all the time stupid question.
I: Oh, really.
Eva: Oh, yeah.
Elsa: Sometime he [Chris] have stupid question for Amy, because you know Amy is young. [He asked about] Boyfriend or?
Eva: And then later coming one guy and every time he sit here-
I: Sit here?
Eva: Yeah, and the he and the Amy sometimes play, maybe that Chris one question.

Elsa: It's because sometimes you know, she's nice. Teacher Amy is nice and she's young, and smile and just happy. When the guy sometimes look the teacher no serious or something. I say ah, and sometimes I know hear the guys have stupid question for Amy. For example, [guys] say 'oh, you have a boyfriend?' Oh, wow sometime I remember Amy say, 'no I have a boyfriend'.

I: So, then because this kind of situation, teacher Amy said you're stupid?

Elsa: Yeah, I don't remember and if she said I understand her because the guys sometimes it's stupid question for her. Yeah, if she said this, I understand her.

When I asked Chris about this incident, he seemed not to want to talk more about it, but said it was a joke:

I: I heard that one day, maybe true of not. Teacher Amy said to you stupid?

Chris: Yeah.

I: Is that right?

Chris: It is true.

I: Really, what happened?

Chris: I don't know.

I: Do you remember what happened?

Chris: It was like, say a lot of-

I: She speak a lot?

Chris: Yeah. Better. It was like kidding with me...

I: Kidding?

Chris: Like playing with me.

I: Oh, playing. Okay. Kidding, not serious.

Chris: No.

The word 'stupid' spoken by a teacher seemed to work differently for different individuals, including making a student drop out (Domingo) and making students sympathize (Eva, Elsa). What really happened seems to be that Chris asked an inappropriate question, because two other students witnessed that, and after that night, a man (assuming teacher Amy's friend) came to Amy's class. The fact that the man came to class was also interpreted differently. I recall that, when I visited their church, Fernando (Irma's husband), Irma and other students told me that an American man came to Amy's class and kept talking English to her. Fernando and Irma felt that Amy seemed to not teach them but brought an American man and talked with him in English during their class time. But listening to Eva and Elsa's narratives, it seems that there were reasons behind the scenes, but different people interpreted the situation differently. Thus, teachers should be careful about using an extreme word (e.g.

stupid) under any circumstances, because of potential misunderstandings and subsequent results.

In addition, the participants seem to interpret the speech speed of their English teachers differently. Domingo and Chris interpreted teacher Amy's English speed as fast:

> Amy, the teacher, does not have an idea or time for explain, and only talk, talk and talk so fast (Domingo).

> And I remember when Eva told her, teacher Amy, she speak fast...So fast yeah (Chris).

However, for Eva and Elsa, Amy's talking speed was okay:

I:	So, I was wondering did your teacher, like Derek or Amy say something too fast to you, sometimes?
Eva:	Who?
I:	Amy or Derek, did they speak too fast?
Eva:	No, no.
Elsa:	No, no.
I:	Teachers were okay. Teachers not talking too fast?
Eva and Elsa:	No.

Teacher Derek's speed of English speech was regarded as slow, thus boring for Eva, Elsa, Irma and Chris, but okay for Mag and Domingo:

I:	Derek was slow?
Eva:	Very slow.
Elsa:	For Eva, yeah. Slow.

Irma reported that she learned nothing from teacher Derek, but Mag and Domingo defended Derek by saying they learned something:

> Derek don't bring nothing prepared and he asks about movies, things that mean nothing. And when I see in my notes, my journal. When I see nothing, it mean there is nothing.

Unlike Irma, Mag and Domingo recounted that they learned something from Derek: 'The sounds of the letters, yeah I think. I learned a little bit from Derek'. Domingo even recalled the specifics of what he learned from Derek, the consonants and vowels:

> Yeah, talking only a specific, how, talking. But, you know. I remember Derek like showed letters and sounds and, you know, the, for example, yeah, the vocabulary for the ABC. Consonants. Yeah, consonants. And, you know, when... show letters... Yeah, and long letters and sounds. The vowel? Yeah, exactly. Yeah, it was good. You know.

Theme 10 seems to show that the different perspectives and reactions from students to the same teachers' instructions and input play a significant role in their decisions whether to stay or drop out.

Mapping Out What Makes Adult ELs Drop Out

It seems that the six categories: (1) unrelated topics, (2) no prep, (3) boring, (4) just talk, talk, talk, (5) unmet expectations and (6) different perspectives and reactions dynamically contribute to the dominant three categories of (7) learn nothing, (8) teacher apathy and (9) feeling oppressed. The intertwined relations among these nine categories seem to converge to the feeling of (10) waste of time, which seems to critically lead the participants to drop out by saying 'me no more come'.

Figure 7.1 illustrates the probable network among dropout factors that thematically emerged in this study's findings. The three thick squares with learn nothing, teacher apathy and feeling oppressed mean that the three categories are dominant findings. The six thin squares mean that unrelated topics, just talk, talk, talk, unmet expectations, no prep, boring and different perspectives and reactions work as subcategories supporting the three dominant findings. The arrows drawn from the six thin squares to the three thick squares show the probable causal relationships. For example, unrelated topics seems to make the participants learn nothing, feel not cared about (teacher apathy) and bored. Likewise, the arrows among the subcategories and dominant squares show the probable map of how these findings contribute to the participants' decision process. The arrows connecting the cluster of nine categories on the left to waste of time show the probable causal relation toward the participants' final decisions to drop out.

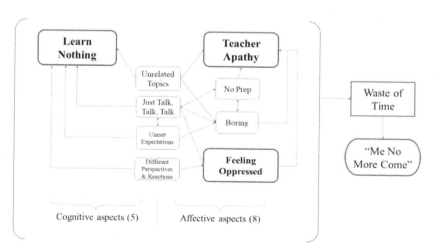

Figure 7.1 Map of what makes the participants drop out

Following constructivism, I uphold that it is hard to dichotomize the cognitive and affective aspects. As another facet of the dropout phenomenon, however, on the bottom of Figure 7.1, I illustrate how the categories converge to either cognitive or affective aspects in the participants' decisions to drop out. It seems that the affective aspects outnumber the cognitive aspects in a ratio of 8:5 when the participants decide to drop out. Specifically, it seems that the four categories in the middle of Figure 7.1 – unrelated topics, just talk, talk, talk, unmet expectation and different perspectives and reactions – can be counted as both cognitive and affective aspects because all four aspects simultaneously seem to contribute to both cognitive (learn nothing) and affective (teacher apathy) aspects. Thus, the frequency counts for each aspect start with 4, then, for the cognitive side, 1 is added by the learn nothing aspect, which makes a total of 5. On the other hand, starting with 4 following the same logic, 4 more are added with teacher apathy, no prep, boring and feeling oppressed, which makes a total of 8. Therefore, it seems that affective aspects played a more critical role in the participants' decisions to drop out. This finding seems to be consistent with Richard-Amato (1988) who argues that L2 learning occurs through both cognitive and affective aspects within one's mind. Further, for this particular case, it is probable to argue that affective domains seem to work more significantly on dropping-out decisions, which would be a meaningful finding for ESL stakeholders.

8 What Makes Adult ELs Stay

Seven categories were reported regarding what makes adult English learners (ELs) decide to stay: good teacher/class, learn something new, good/caring feelings, feedback/homework checking, interesting topics, ease of comprehension and dynamic activities. Among the seven categories, three themes emerged. Theme by theme, what makes adult ELs stay is addressed below.

Theme 11: Good Teacher/Class – Learn Something New – Good/Caring Feelings

The data revealed that the participants seem to want to stay in their EL classes when they have feelings of superación (self-improvement, self-actualization) through having a good teacher/class, notions that were supported by their feelings of learning something new and good/caring feelings.

Good teacher/class

Irma recounted that teacher John is a good teacher for her, because she perceived that he helps her to improve her English. Irma felt bad about the fact that her English is not good enough even though she has lived in the US for about 27 years. To Irma, teacher John is a good teacher because he helps her superación, so she wants to stay in this teacher's class:

> I say, oh my gosh 27 years and no correct English. But I remember about I say, oh John, John is a good teacher and I need John back and learn and English.

When I asked what makes Irma think teacher John is a good teacher, Irma pointed out that John has passion. By having passion, what Irma seems to mean is that she feels teacher John cares about the students compared to other teachers:

Irma: Has passion, yeah. John has passion.

I: And then for example, in another way, so in comparison, you think teacher Derek has no passion, is that right?

Irma: No, I think Derek is, only he want talk like, like me no really English. He think maybe, I know a lot of English like, talk and talk and talk.

I: Ah.

Irma: Maybe Derek, he have another student learn more of me, I guess is why he talk and talk and talk. Not like you, because like teacher John know how many English I know. You [teacher John] know how many English Domingo have. And you know Eva and every-body for one and one and one. You know how many English we got and you know how many help we need. It's why I like it to do with John, because the other people maybe have no very interest. No got a lot interest how many English, how much English I have. Yeah and when I start English, my English class with you, I feel Superación, I feel very, really comfortable. Very comfortable and because I say oh, John say this is not pronounced like that, okay, let me do better. And it's why I like you John. It's why.

Lastly, Irma reported that when teacher John gives corrective feedback, she feels that he is interested in helping people, through loving his job. This feeling seems to make Irma think that teacher John is a good teacher:

Irma: Uh-huh and you correcting everybody and we feel better because somebody is interested in my English. Somebody, you have this, you know how, you say 'okay let me help you'. You want every-body help, you like, you like, you love your job, you like your job when you show other people.

I: So you can feel that?

Irma: Yeah, I feel like that. I feel that. Yeah, I feel when, when you teach English, I can feel that you want help me and Domingo, and Mag and everybody.

For Domingo, teacher Derek and teacher John were both good teach-ers. Domingo thought teacher Derek a quiet but good teacher because Domingo learned something new from him such as consonants and vow-els, as reported earlier:

Yeah, he's [Derek] good. Good, good teacher. Yeah. Little quiet. Not talking too much. Good teacher.

Domingo seems to think that teacher John is a good teacher because he explains things well, helping Domingo understand better. Domingo recalled that during a break time, he talked to other classmates about this feeling:

Mhmm. Well, because it's a, 'Oh, this is good teacher. Explain very good. It's very good idea what you're talking'.

For Eva and Mag, having a good teacher seems to make them more willing to accommodate time conflicts. At the very beginning of their interviews, they said being busy is the reason for dropping out, but after a while, they said they can accommodate their schedule if they have a good teacher:

> If teacher John start to teach English up again I can try to come. (Mag)

> Some time I can go, for my friend, ask Delma [Eva's daughter]. I can say 'Delma, Delma you take care of this baby, I go to class'. (Eva)

For Elsa, teacher John was a good teacher because Elsa understood what he taught, and he gave homework and used many examples. Elsa thinks he told her 'everything' she needs to know:

Elsa: Teacher John class is good. You know that they, you no need to change nothing, you are good teacher. You're very good teacher. After you left, everybody left. You make homework, you're good teacher.

Elsa: I understand you, you have good examples, you have good examples.

I: Good examples, okay. Examples good.

Elsa: You talk, you talk everything.

For Chris, instructing with group-work activities made teacher John's class a good class. And Chris said he was happy and felt like a family in John's class, which seems to make Chris feel that John is a good teacher:

> You're a good teacher because you... for that two hours class, work in group...your class is like family and happy, always happy right here.

All six participants reported that a good teacher/class matters. Whether the teacher or class is good for their superación is a critical factor in their decision to stay or drop out. Specifically, when they felt they had learned something new, it seems that it was worth staying in the class. Also, they seem to continuously evaluate, share and monitor the characteristics of the feelings in a classroom about whether or not the teacher cares about students' superación.

Learn something new

The participants reported that they learn something new, which makes them feel that their teacher is a good teacher, thus they want to stay. Irma, for example, felt that she had learned something new when she learned how to make a question in English by saying 'excuse me, I have a question'. Irma thought that it is very important to make a question, which in turn seems to lead her to keep learning more English:

Irma: Yeah.

I: So how do you think about that feeling, 'Now I know how to ask a question', is it important or is it good?

Irma: Oh, it's really important.

I: Okay, can you tell me more about that? How do you feel about that?

Irma: I feel more comfortable, and more safety and more respect. I feel better when I say 'excuse me', because I understand 'excuse me' is a really good word. Really good word. Really good. Yeah, I learned here.

I: Yeah,

Irma: And, yeah, when I understand that word is important, I want more, and learn more English.

Mag also recounted that she had learned something new such as making a question for daily conversations: '[I learned] How are you doing today, in your class?'. Domingo felt that he had learned something new about how to say the past and future tense. To Domingo, learning about the English future tense seems very meaningful because he recounted that he changed his vision based on that learning:

Domingo: When you come over here, that's..., you know. Because, for example, right now I use the, before, you know? Before, yesterday is before, right? And all the time before and no future. No, right now I'm talking about future. You know, I change my vision of things, change my mind, and focus on something future.

I: For future.

Domingo: Yeah.

I: Oh. For example, maybe?

Domingo: For example, I use, use the one, I don't know. All the time before, like 'I did it before, I did these before. Before'. But, right now, I change my vision, for future.

I: For future. For example, 'I will', maybe?

Domingo: Yes, 'I will', this one.

I: You change your mind from the class?

Domingo: Yeah. Simple, I give it to the book before and I don't know how, how to speak in future. You know? Before, I don't know how to speak in the future. But now sometimes my vision, the future, you know?

I: Oh, okay.

Domingo: My mind and know because everything is better in the future. But the past is past, you know? It's nothing, the time in the past.

Lastly, Elsa said that she would stay in her English class if she learns at least one word a day. Although other people might think learning one word is not enough, Elsa recounted that she can learn many words in one year if she can learn one word per day:

Elsa: I want to go to learn, if me learn one word, in the class it's good for me.

I: Okay.

Elsa: In the next class, maybe learn too much but if me learn one word it's good for me. One word, if me learn one word every day I say many words learn one year.

I: Yeah, yeah one year, right.

Elsa: In one year. But many people think different, other people may think learn nothing [if they learn only one word a day], [they may think] it's boring. And I say 'okay, but me go to English class'.

Good/caring feelings

In addition to the feeling of learning something new, the participants reported that they value good/caring feelings from teachers, which make them stay. For example, Mag reported that she feels better with teacher John than with the other teachers: 'I feel better with you, like I learned'. For Domingo, having a good feeling between the teacher and himself seems important. Domingo kept saying that he had 'no feeling' with the other teachers. It turns out that Domingo seeks a caring feeling from teachers:

I: What do you mean by feeling?

Domingo: Feeling, no, no. Teacher have no feeling.

I: To me or?

Domingo: No, teacher Amy. Amy, no feeling with him. With she.

I: With her?

Domingo: With her. Mhmm.

I: So, no feeling?

Domingo: No feeling. No like, only talking.

I asked Doming more about what he meant by having feeling. He said having feeling means having a good/nice/caring feeling similar to feelings that he can have with his friends. That kind of nice feeling was absent with teacher Amy, as Amy said 'hurry up' to Domingo when he copied words and sentences the teacher had written on the whiteboard into his notebook:

I:	Just talking.
Domingo:	talking and.
	....
I:	So, there's no feeling.
Domingo:	No feeling.
I:	The feeling, but to other teachers, you have feeling?
Domingo:	Sure. Feeling like a nice person, you know. Like, you said in class, 'take your time' and it's more relaxed. You know like because the people get nervous when they start something new. For, you know, and then when somebody tell you 'hurry up', you're like more nervous for, you know.
I:	So what do you mean by feeling?
Domingo:	Well, I think feeling, feeling is nice. Nice feeling, you know, like when, with my person or you, you know, my friends. Nice and good, feeling good guy with other people.
I:	Okay, good.
Domingo:	Yes. Like good person. Good friend. You know, like relaxed, happy. And you know, smile, you know like, 'Hey, how are you?' you know? Talking with other. Yeah. But, no, teacher Amy no feeling like that.

Lastly, Eva, Elsa and Chris felt so welcomed in teacher John's class that they wanted to stay. For example, when I gave Elsa a 0–10 scale to describe how she felt welcomed, she gave 11 for teacher John, 7 for Amy and 4 for Derek. To sum up, learning something new and feeling good and caring seemed to make the participants feel that this is a good teacher/class for their superación, so that they wanted to stay.

Theme 12: Feedback/Homework Checking – Interesting Topics – Ease of Comprehension

The students also wanted to stay when they received feedback/ homework checking and when the class covered interesting topics, both of which support their comprehension of the class content.

Feedback/homework checking

First, all participants seem to value corrective feedback and home-work checking provided by teachers. Corrective feedback either in class or through checking homework seems to play a significant role, leading the participants to stay and keep learning. For example, Irma recounted that teacher John showed them how to pronounce English sounds such as the 'th' sound, by demonstrating where the tongue should be located and how it should move for appropriate pronunciation. This teaching method seemed new and effective to her compared to other teachers in the past:

> For example, you [teacher John] show how to pronounce correctly and you show do that. You show me and everybody how to move tongue that time. Other teachers don't do that, no. I have [teachers] in the past. I have two or three teachers in the USA but they no show me [their tongues to teach pronunciation] like teacher John.

Specifically, Irma recalled that when teacher John walked around while they were participating in a group discussion, John listened and corrected her English. Irma seems to think that corrective feedback is important to her English learning:

> When teacher John make a little groups and you come, you walk around everybody. You hear how I pronounce my English and you see how other people pronounce their English and you say 'no, no, no like that', and you correcting everybody. And we feel better because somebody is interested in Superación for my English. Somebody, you have this. He is like, he know how, say 'okay let me help' and you want help everybody.

Domingo also recounted the importance of corrective feedback in class for his learning. Domingo said that when he talks and practices English without receiving feedback, he doesn't know whether his English is correct. But English teachers' corrective feedback helped him, so he changed and learned:

> When [I] talk, this is not correct, and you [teacher] talk, this is correct. And, the way sometimes no speak English because 'oh, I don't say this correctly'. Yeah, it's like, I think it's not correct, you know? When you come over here in the class, 'oh, okay, say that, this is correct'. You know? I changed my English because I talking more better, more correct.

Because in-class feedback can occur through interactions between teachers and students, it is important to have a class culture where students are willing to ask teachers questions. Mag said that nobody asked any questions in teacher Amy's class, which may imply that there was a lack of feedback in Amy's class: 'Nobody raise their hand for making question, nobody, no questions'.

Eva and Elsa recounted that checking homework is important, because they learn from a teacher's feedback. Elsa reported that teacher John checks her homework either on Monday or Wednesday, which seems good for her learning because she can receive feedback:

So, you say this on Monday, 'okay this is the homework of today'. I think, 'homework okay'. Then on Wednesday you check. You say 'okay you come you check, okay this is no good, this is good', everything check.

Eva also recounted that a teacher's active homework checking matters. Eva brought her homework home and completed it outside of her busy daily routines, thus checking by the teacher seems meaningful for her learning:

Eva: Yes, you check homework for everybody.
I: Homework.
Eva: Yeah. I have homework, okay yeah check this in my home, I know how much time, I take.
I: I know, right.
Eva: And then Monday, and then Monday I put in the table, maybe on Wednesday, [I think] 'oh, class'. Yeah, and you check the homework. Good.

Interesting topics – ease of comprehension

Along with receiving corrective feedback, having interesting topics related to their life is regarded as important in the participants' decisions to stay, and enables ease of comprehension of the class contents. For example, Irma reported that she can learn English more effectively by using life-related topics and daily conversations. She critiqued the use of unrelated topics such as movies: 'No, only the movies, they never see the movie, so I can't say about the movie I never see. But my story, I can speak'. Further, Irma specifically mentioned the topics related to her life that she can actively talk about in English and learn through:

Irma: Yeah, I like it. When you start [talking] about my day, [by saying] 'how was your day, what did you do this morning, and what you do this afternoon?' What do you next, when you start the story about my passion, I learn more. Yeah.
I: Do you remember any examples?
Irma: Yeah, when you say 'what, how was your morning today', I say 'well this morning I went to the store, okay this afternoon I go to the shopping uh, tonight I go to my daughter house'.
I: And then you learn more.
Irma: Yeah, I learn more. More when we, when we study about my life.
I: That's true, but other teachers maybe-
Irma: No, the other teachers don't make nothing about my life story. My life or the other life or the other stories. No I don't think so.
I: The movie maybe.
Irma: No, only the movies. I never see the movie, so I can't say about the movies. I never see. But my story, I can speak. Yeah, I can speak

about my story, about the story about my grandchildren. I can do that, but not the other things.

This daily-life conversation-based learning topic was shared by Mag's report too. Mag recounted when she learned a daily conversation English expression: '[I learned] How was your day today, your class?'. Also, one night we used the US government's policy on immigration under President Trump when we practiced two verbs – agree and disagree. Mag recalled that discussion as the topic seemed to be related to her life.

I: Right, 'agree'. You remember that word, like 'yeah I agree with you'. You remember that, when we use the example, President?

Mag: Yeah. Donald Trump. I learn agree and disagree.

Having an interesting class seems to matter to the participants' decisions about whether to stay or drop out. Elsa recounted that if she found the class not interesting, she would stay home. On the other hand, when the class is interesting, she would come and stay in the class:

Sometimes because I saw the teacher is no good, and class is not interesting, I said no. I lose my time, I prefer staying in my home and relax or watch TV or stay here. Sometimes I am tired or something, or I need to make things or go to the store, or something. Sometimes I say, no, cause my time right here, I say no I prefer to stay in my home. But, when the teacher, the class is interesting, I say go, I learn English.

When I asked Eva and Elsa if they wanted to come to the English class, regardless of who teaches, they said they would only come for interesting and good teachers but not for other teachers.

I: So if you have class now and you want to come?

Eva: Yes.

I: Um, no matter who teaches?

Elsa: No, the reason I drop out is, because the class is different and teacher Amy and other teacher. When teacher John here, everybody goes listen and pay attention because John class was very good. I think Eva and I take class many years before, but when I took to Eva say, 'teacher John a more better teacher than all the years taking English class'. When all the teachers come, everybody laugh, talk,

Eva: Play.

Elsa: Uh-huh, in teacher John class everybody listen and pay attention, because your class is interesting. It's, I liked it.

What Eva and Elsa meant by interesting seems to have two meanings: (1) the class/topics are related to their life/needs and (2) they learn something new from it, inferring from other students' narratives. The other four students' meaning of interesting seemed to converge on these two concepts as well. Likewise, Domingo recounted that an interesting class is important to his life. For example, he recalled that learning vocabulary words about housing construction items (table, lamp, bedrooms, etc.) was very meaningful to him and that he learned a lot from it:

Domingo:	And sometimes then my boss... wants me go a bedroom. And I remember when you teach.
I:	Bedroom and other words.
Domingo:	Yeah, the paper, you know, like, table, lamp, and all this stuff. I think 'Oh, okay, it's this'. But before I had no idea.
I:	So, you want to know that.
Domingo:	Yeah.
I:	That's good.
Domingo:	Yeah, this is good for me.

Teaching housing vocabulary terms was coincidently designed because I believed that the terms would be useful for the students' daily lives (Figure 8.1). But I didn't expect that learning the terms would be beneficial for Domingo's work. Likewise, Chris brought up and connected life-related topics to his English learning, which seemed important to his English learning. For example, during the interview, Chris asked how to describe his work as a concrete builder. Once I had given him

---

Listen and Repeat

Bedroom	Bathroom	Living Room	Kitchen
a bed	a bathtub	a sofa	a table
a dresser	a toilet	a television	a stove
a mirror	a sink	a coffee table	a refrigerator
a lamp	a shower	a cabinet	a counter

Complete the Sentences

1. In my bedroom, I have _____, _____, and _____.
2. In my bathroom, I have _____, _____, and _____.
3. In my living room, I have _____, _____, and _____.
4. In my kitchen, I have _____, _____, and _____.

Figure 8.1 The textbook example we used to learn about housing vocabulary (author created). This class seemed meaningful to Domingo's life because he learned the terms useful for his construction work

an example sentence such as 'I'm here to...', Chris made four different sentences:

I: That's a good practice
Chris: Yes, good practice, see. I am going to learn to talk more better and,
I: Yeah, you can say 'hi mister, I'm here, I'm here to make the pool'.
Chris: Yeah.
I: I'm here to... I'm here to is good. You can say that. Can you say that?
Chris: What?
I: I'm here.
Chris: I'm here to do a concrete.
I: Yeah. Yeah, that's good.
Chris: I'm... I'm the concrete guy...
I: Good.
Chris: And I come and do the concrete.
I: That's good.
Chris: Can you tell me... can you tell me where you want to pour the concrete?

Interesting and life-related topics/class that simultaneously enables ease of comprehension seem important to the participants when they decide to stay or drop out, because the connections between their class time and their life/work seem to support their decision to invest. As Elsa reported, once the time invested in their English class is not worthwhile, the participants seemed to subtract their investment (time and energy) immediately by dropping out. Rather, if the connection is alive, it seems that they want to stay.

Theme 13: Dynamic Activities

Lastly, the interview data revealed that the participants have a desire to participate in dynamic activities for their learning (group work, presentations, learning with music and practicing sounds using their tongue), which, when met, leads them to stay because the dynamic activities help them comprehend, thus the class is interesting. For example, Irma reported that she likes group work because she can share ideas and practice with her peers:

Yeah, I like it, group work. Because we trade, ask. And I hear the other people how you say, and how me say, and how say the teacher. [I learned] 'Oh, okay, it's not right'. And we can practice.

Chris also likes group work and making presentations standing up: 'When it was like... and the class, I like in group I had to stand up'. For

Mag, a dynamic activity would be explicit verbal practice of sentences between the teacher and students, and among students too.

Mag: [I like verbal] Repeat, repeat, repeat.
I: Practice.
Mag: Practice.
Mag: I like how you [teacher John] teach because you make a question and they answer by, if they don't speak, you'll repeat it again and so we practice.
I: Practice.
Mag: I like how you teach. Yeah practice, practice sentences with teacher and practice with friends.

Domingo also pointed out that he likes to practice. To him, copying teachers' writing on a whiteboard seems good practice:

> You write a sentence for us and then the peoples copy the sentence and make same. Yeah, I like practice the example.

The value of practice seems to apply not only to writing, but also to how to make phonetic sounds. Eva pointed out that teacher John taught her pronunciation by showing tongue placement. It seems that she felt this practice was useful for her learning. Eva recounted that she learned how to pronounce '-pare' with the word 'prepare'. Eva said, 'yeah and then you help, and then you help for the pronunciation... now with this word. I said prep before, now I know it's prepare'. Likewise, Irma said that practicing pronunciation by showing tongue placement is a good activity, a notion she pointed out when we talked about her preferences over group work. Irma seems to recall that we practiced the sound differences between 'th' and 'd' and voiced (g) and un-voiced consonants (k):

Irma: The group work. We listen and you,
I: Group work, listen and um-
Irma: And you show how to move the tongue.
I: Show how move the tongue. For sounds of 'th' and 'd'.
Irma: And how, how the pronounce, how you feel in the [Irma pointed out her neck].
I: In your neck.
Irma: Uh-huh.
I: Throat. [for voiced/unvoiced consonants]
Irma: Yeah I like it, I like the sound practice with groups.

It seems that the participants want dynamic activities for their English learning, because it is more effective than just sitting and listening. It seems that the two reasons behind this preference are (1) students come to class when physically tired and (2) they have different learning backgrounds. For example, when the class is boring without dynamic activities, thus when there is no learning, Elsa said she would stop and go home to rest. Chris also said that he is tired, so he wants to actively learn by having group work or standing up and presenting ideas. Active interactions between teacher and students, and among students, seem to work as a dynamic activity too, as Mag recounted. Including dynamic activities seemed to work as another vehicle supporting the adult ELs' decisions to stay.

Mapping Out What Makes Adult ELs Stay

It seems that the seven categories work together in an intertwined way to influence participants' decisions to stay in EL classes. First, the feelings of learning something new and good/caring feelings seem to make the participants think that the teacher/class is good and helping their superación. Thus, they want to stay. The other four categories (feedback/homework checking, ease of comprehension, dynamic activities and interesting topics) seem to support the first two dominant categories (learning something new, good/caring feelings). These categories are not static but rather living. For example, Eva said that supporting Delma (Eva's daughter) was her top priority a few years prior to this study and was equal to her superación. However, Eva acknowledged that at the time when this study was conducted, her priority was her own development. She put her own self-improvement as her top priority, as a current form of her superación. This finding is consistent with the notions of fluidity and dynamic-ness of identity and capital based on space and time (Darvin & Norton, 2015). The factors for adult EL's investment in English learning are strongly connected to their situation, which is diverse and evolves over time.

Figure 8.2 illustrates a probable map among the seven categories. The thick squares with learn something new, good/caring feelings and good teacher/class mean that these are the three dominant categories working together toward making the participants feel that this class is helping their superación, thereby supporting their desire to stay. Under learn something new and good/caring feelings, four thin squares display the sub-categories of feedback/homework checking, ease of comprehension, dynamic activities and interesting topics. The arrows from feedback/ homework checking to learn something new, good/caring feelings and ease of comprehension show the probable causal relations among these four categories. The arrows from dynamic activities, interesting topics to ease of comprehension also show the probable causal relationships between these categories.

Along with the continuum of cognitive and affective domains of second language acquisition (SLA) at the bottom of Figure 8.2, I illustrate

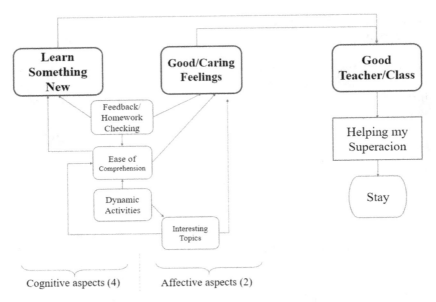

Figure 8.2 Map of what makes adult ELs at the CEL decide to stay

how the categories converge in either cognitive or affective aspects in the participants' decisions to stay. Contrary to the dropout factors, it seems that the cognitive aspects outnumber the affective aspects when the participants decide to stay at a ratio of 4:2. Specifically, learn something new, feedback/homework checking, ease of comprehension and dynamic activities seem to contribute to the learners' cognitive perceptional aspects in their learning, whereas good/caring feelings and interesting topics seem to contribute to the learners' affective aspects in learning. Eventually, all six categories co-influence the learners' feeling of good teacher/class that helps their superación, and thus their decision to stay. As this illustration depicts, it seems that adult ELs in the CEL decide to stay in their class based on these multiple and interrelating factors.

9 Discussion

Adult ELs: Problem-Solvers with Resilience toward Social Justice

This study found that the adult English learners (ELs) at the Center for English Literacy (CEL) are problem-solvers. The data revealed that all six participants proactively solved many problems in their lives with creativity and persistence. For example, Domingo's extensive knowledge and experiences of repairing cars showed that he improvised using non-standard tools, such as lumber instead of a jack-stand. He never seemed to stop moving. I often wondered how his persistent efforts on his cars played into his English learning. Irma evolved, stepping into a translator role at the factory to aid communication between the workers and her boss. Eva and Elsa solved their language barrier problems at their job by continuously attending local EL classes as much as possible. Mag also tried to solve her problems with English, highlighted by her disastrous trip to hospital, by attending local EL classes. Chris kept solving his daily language barrier problems at work by talking to his girlfriend in English and attending local EL classes. Irma, Domingo and Chris' proactive problem-solving approaches led to a separate Sunday English class. This persistent problem-solving skill is consistent with the notion of intelligence in life that scholars have found in adult workers' intellectual and creative behaviors while performing their jobs (Carraher, 1986; Carraher *et al.*, 1985; Resnick, 1987; Rose, 2001, 2005). Adult ELs showed persistence and enthusiasm, even under less than ideal conditions. When I look back on the challenges they faced, it is astounding that they had any energy left to attend English classes. English language teachers for refugee and immigrant groups should not underestimate the desire for investment and the problem-solving skills of their students. The task is to help adult ELs apply their problem-solving skills, which are very active in their lives, to learning English.

Resilience against oppression

The adult ELs in the CEL seem to possess high resilience during their journey to a new world, language and culture. They came to the US and have lived here for 13+ years on average, despite language barriers at work and within their families and communities, and the numerous risks of being deported. Their family support responsibilities and the feeling of more rewards in the US seem to lead them to invest in living in the US to achieve a better future for their family and themselves. Along the way, many hardships occurred such as losing her spouse (Irma), children become ill (Domingo, Mag, Eva, Elsa) and being silent and oppressed by fast English-speaking colleagues and bosses (Mag, Eva, Elsa, Domingo, Chris, Irma). However, in the end, these hardships seem to play a positive role in their pursuit of English learning. When I look at those hardships and how they dealt with them, I found their natural desire to speak up against oppression (Freire, 1976, 1996, 1998). One reason behind all of these phenomena, such as border crossing, continuing to work hard labor jobs for a better future and continuing to knock down doors in the English as a second language (ESL) classrooms, could be that they don't want to remain oppressed by materialistic, mental and ideological pressures. For example, Mag, Domingo and Chris reported that they can earn good money based on their working hours in the US, but that is not the case in Mexico. Eva and Elsa recounted that regardless of how smart you are, you can't continue education in Mexico because everything is expensive and economic capital is not shared. Only a few people are privileged. It seems that adult ELs maintain strong resilience against daily social oppression along with their continued risk-taking and ongoing survival in the US.

The Voices Explored: Superación, Push and Proactive Investment

Superación: Major factor for investment and staying

When it comes to the decision to invest and stay, the seven categories (see Figure 8.2) seem to support participants' decision about whether 'this teacher/class is good for helping my superación'. Using Darvin and Norton's (2015) investment framework, I found that the superación notion can be broken down into three specific constructs: capital, identity and ideology. The participants seem to set superación up front when they evaluate a teacher/class in terms of staying or dropping out. It seems that they ask the following questions: 'Does this teacher/class help me gain economic capital (income, promotion), cultural capital (knowledge, educational credential) and social capital (network with people in power)? Does this teacher/class help me to better position myself within English-speaking conversation sites? Does this teacher/class respect my ideological background and help me to stand up with equal access to mainstream ideology?'. Under the term superación, it seems that the students simultaneously and in multilayered ways evaluate their teacher and class. When these expectations are met, it seems that they want to stay or vice versa.

Specifically, the three categories of learn something new, receiving corrective feedback/homework checking and ease of comprehension can be viewed as gaining cultural capital (knowledge and educational credentials), through which the participants feel that they can gain further economic capital (promotion) and social capital (network with other people in power) in the future. For example, Domingo called what he learned in the class 'information', which seems to show the probable link between the knowledge he learns in class and the value of such knowledge as capital. This capital can give Domingo affordances to enable him to position himself with the right to speak, thus he would positively negotiate his identity through such capital (e.g. Domingo can confidently translate between his boss and his colleagues at work). In turn, this link between earning capital and negotiating identity can help Domingo to transform his ideology by empowering him to achieve better positioning and overcome the systemic patterns of control (losing chances of conversations, practice, thus chances of gaining capital). Superación, dominantly reported in this study, seems to work dynamically among capital, identity and ideology, because when needs based on these are met, it seems the students feel that the class is good for their superación.

The fluid and dynamic nature of superación

For adult ELs at the CEL, a major factor for their investment in English learning is their desire for superación, in other words becoming a better person, self-improvement and self-actualization. This finding is consistent with Dewey (1903) who pointed out that the purpose of education is the self-actualization of each individual based on one's discursive and idiosyncratic needs and goals. The superación's specific colors and shapes were different among all six participants, and more importantly, it kept evolving over time based on their current situation. It seems that English language stakeholders, teachers, administrators and fundraisers might think that adult ELs need to learn English for their daily functions such as grocery shopping and work. Those immediate needs were reported. However, all the participants reported that becoming a better person was their top reason to invest in English language learning.

As discussed, the specific forms of each individual's superación were different, such as being able to advise their children for the future in English (Domingo), protecting their children using English (Irma), becoming a better person (Mag), becoming a fast English listener and speaker (Eva), becoming a college student (Elsa) and becoming a better person at work (Chris). It is worthwhile noting that adult ELs are eager to improve themselves through learning the English language, thus their motivation is generally high (Bernat, 2004; Derwing, 2003; Hyman, 2002; Valentine, 1990). However, it seems plausible to differentiate mental motivation and actual investment, because high motivation does not guarantee actual learning all the time (Darvin & Norton, 2015; Gearing & Peter, 2018; Norton, 2012). Eventually, 19 out of 20 students dropped out in this book's context (Chris only remained for his probation requirement). This phenomenon seems to support the distinction between motivation and investment notions. Further, in this case, whether the teacher/class was helping their superación was a critical criterion for the participants' decision.

It would be worthwhile adapting this investment framework when assessing a teacher's instruction practices, developing student satisfaction surveys and evaluating the impact of EL programs. On the other hand, when these constructs are missing, it seems that the classes and teachers push the students out of the class (Doll *et al.*, 2013).

Push: Major Factor for Adult ELs' Drop Out

Revisiting the inductive findings of this study with the Doll *et al.* (2013) framework of push, pull and fall out, it seems that the majority of dropout factors for adult ELs at the CEL can be categorized as push. Push factors refer to any pressures occurring inside the classroom that 'push' students out of the class. It seems that all 10 categories of dropout factors that emerged in this study are based on what happened inside the classroom: learn nothing, teacher apathy, feeling oppressed, unrelated topics, just talk-talk-talk, unmet expectations, different perspectives and reactions, no prep, boring and the feeling of waste of time. The 10 categories seem to be consistent with the push factor's characteristics (Doll *et al.*, 2013).

Compared to the push factors for high school students reported by Doll *et al.* (2013), the specific forms of push factors for adult ELs were different. One reason would be the students different situatedness (Gee, 2012, 2014; Wenger, 1998). While low grades, attendance issues and discipline problems are push factors for high school students, students' feeling of learning nothing, no caring and oppression from their teachers/classes are push factors in this particular context. Therefore, to Doll *et al.*'s (2013) list, affective and emotional domains such as teacher apathy can be added.

Another distinctive feature this study found is that, for adult ELs, push factors play a more important role than pull and fall out. Doll *et al.* (2013) found that for high school students' dropout decision, pull factors were the major causes such as having a job or getting married. As Gee (2012, 2014) and Lave and Wenger (1991) recounted, it seems that adult ELs' unique situatedness foregrounds the finding that push factors played a major role in this particular context. In fact, pull factors such as babysitting during class hours (Eva) and losing weight for her daughter's quinceañera preparation (Elsa) were reported, but were less often cited. During her interview, Eva told me that she could accommodate the babysitting schedule with another family member so that she could go to class, as long as the teacher/class was good for her superación. This shows that pull factors might be at work in the adult ELs' decision processes, but the adult ELs at the CEL seem to be capable of minimizing the pull factors to continue their investment.

Caring Matters

One unexpected thematic finding was the students' emphasis on 'caring'. All the participants reported that they left the class (except Chris who was required to stay for his probation) because they thought the teachers didn't care about them. For example, Irma saw that teacher Derek didn't prepare for the class and thus did not care about the students. Mag, Eva, Elsa, Chris and Domingo all felt that teachers Amy and Derek didn't care whether or not they learned, understood or followed the instruction contents. What they saw was that their teachers just talked, talked and talked. Elsa pointed out that the teacher said, 'it is not important' to Elsa's questions, and Elsa said '...but I see the teacher's attitude (for not caring about me)'. The importance of caring is consistent with Noddings' (2013) argument about the importance of teachers' caring. The role of teachers is not only to transmit pieces of knowledge, but also to care for their students as human beings in order to facilitate their learning and empower them, and thus society. Interestingly, the adult students in this study seem to know the value of caring by nature, and they use this concept as one of the criteria for their decisions to stay or drop out. Considering each class has its own culture (Bruner, 1996), teacher apathy seemed to influence students' perceptions of class quality. Caring seems as important as content knowledge.

Other Facets of the Unheard Voices

Silent battles in educational ideologies

Another finding that happened behind the scenes was the silent battle among different educational ideologies between teachers and students. It seems that students' dominant educational ideology is learner centered (Schiro, 2013), which emphasizes self-actualization as the purpose of education. Under a learner-centered (LC) ideology, any topics or contents that individual students are interested in are important, because LC ideology values each individual's idiosyncratic learning interests and topics – and thus the student's growth. All six participants reported that they learn better when it comes to life-related topics. For example, Irma recounted that she can learn better when it comes to the topics of daily life, her grandchildren and jobs. Domingo also recounted that he learned a lot and made connections between his class and his life when he learned vocabulary words and expressions for housing.

However, teachers Derek and Amy's ideologies seemed close to scholar academic (SA) ideology (Schiro, 2013). Derek taught academic pieces of English phonics such as consonants and vowels. He brought up a 'life-related' topic of movies, but it didn't seem to match the particular sociocultural context of the students. As Irma said, she has never watched a movie in the US. Teacher Amy seemed to use many game activities learned through professional development sessions. For example, the Mafia game can be good for students' listening skill development, but the context was not authentic for students' real-life situations. Thus, the practices via the games seemed far removed from the students' real-life interest, which caused the instructional method to remain within the boundary of SA ideology – defined and approved by scholar groups (professional development seminar participants), but not shared by real students.

A muted conflict rages due to students' unforeseen social reconstruction (SR) ideology (Schiro, 2013). Superación – becoming a better person – can be interpreted as transforming students' real lives. For example, Eva wanted to become a fast English speaker and listener, Domingo wanted to build his own construction business by improving his English. Both examples entail reconstructing Eva and Domingo's social positioning. To make it happen, learners already knew that they needed to learn 'correct' English, which could be achieved through epistemologically deep interactions, feedback and practices. However, when teachers Derek and Amy taught peripheral information only, such as grammar and phonics without a context that could connect to students' lives, students interpreted their actions to mean that the teachers did not care. Learners could not see the value of such peripheral fluff for their superación, i.e. transforming toward SR in their lives. Perceived lack of caring led them to quit. This finding is consistent with Tickle (2000), who argued that there are two types of teachers: (1) technicians who protect and reproduce the social status quo and (2) reflective teachers who are agents for social transformation. The consequences of ideologies – social reproduction and social reconstruction – can be profound.

Probable interplay between cognitive and affective aspects

Aside from the primary findings, this study's findings revealed that both cognitive and affective aspects influence students' decisions to stay or drop out. This finding is consistent with second language acquisition scholars who advocate that learning a second language is influenced by the wide variety of components in one's learning such as behavioristic, cognitive, psychological and affective aspects (Arnold, 2011; Krashen, 1982; Lightbown & Spada, 2013; Richard-Amato, 1988). Although both cognitive and affective aspects work together to lead the participants' decisions, this book found that there is a probable distinctive weight between the two aspects when they decide to stay or drop out. For staying factors, it seems that cognitive aspects (such as learning something new, receiving corrective feedback) play more of a role than affective aspects, as depicted in Figure 8.2. On the contrary, for dropping-out factors, affective aspects (such as teacher apathy, feeling oppressed) seem to play a bigger role than cognitive factors (see Figure 7.1). Although both cognitive and affective aspects play important roles together in students' decision-making process, it seems affective aspects are more crucial in pushing out students, eventually leading them to stop their investment.

10 Implications and Conclusion

Reflecting on the findings of this study, I have five implications for English as a second language (ESL) stakeholders: (1) needed paradigm shift, (2) transforming teacher training, (3) supporting the teacher as an ethnographer, (4) transforming case context and (5) suggested use of questionnaires to help the teacher's reflections.

Needed Paradigm Shift: Ecological Approach in Second Language Acquisition

As shown throughout the data and narratives, adult English learners (ELs) desire more organic and ecological approaches to second language (L2) learning. For decades, in the second language acquisition (SLA) field, a myriad of research has been conducted on how to effectively teach content knowledge, such as how to teach grammar structures, how to teach vocabulary through games, how to teach ESL writing skills and so forth (Larsen-Freeman, 1997; Lightbown & Spada, 2013; Swain, 2005). However, such rigorous approaches are useless if our students drop out of their classes. This book shows that affective aspects in L2 learning are as important as how to teach the content knowledge; the affective aspects include, but are not limited to, learners' sociopolitical concerns, psychological aspects, cultural considerations, learner identity, investment and social responsibility of English teaching. In the same vein, SLA scholars have devised an ecological approach to SLA that integrates the complex nature of L2 learning, called the transdisciplinary framework (Costa & Norton, 2017; Douglas Fir Group, 2016). As briefly mentioned in Chapter 2, the Douglas Fir Group, composed of renowned SLA scholars such as Merrill Swain, Bonny Norton and Diane Larsen-Freeman, revealed and emphasized the multifaceted nature of language learning and teaching (see Figure 2.2). The nature of L2 learning is multifaceted, multilayered and consistently evolving over time. It consists of the macro level of ideological structures (belief systems, culture values), the meso level of sociocultural institutions and communities (social identities, families, place of work) and the micro level of social activities (individual engaging with semiotic resources). The investment framework adapted in this study is located in the meso-level layer of social identities. This shows the 'interplay-ability' that one's investment decision may have across the multiple layers of one's L2 learning. One point is that L2 educators and stakeholders should shift their paradigm from only thinking about how to teach content knowledge (semiotic recourses in this model) to broader approaches to address students' ideological structures and social identities in instruction. In practice, ESL teachers and stakeholders should question whether their instructions and curricular support these multilayers in plausible ways to validate students' complex nature of L2 learning.

Transforming Teacher Training

This book's findings show that affective aspects such as caring, oppression and ideological mismatch play a role in L2 students' decisions to invest. However, this topic has been rarely discussed or taught in regular teacher training programs such as master's in teaching English to speakers of other languages (MA TESOL) programs, or in professional development agendas. For example, an MA TESOL program in a US university consists of nine classes that focus on how to teach content knowledge in SLA, such as SLA theory for ESL, ESL methods, phonetics for ESL, structure of the English language, general linguistics for ESL, ESL curriculum, internship in TESOL, teaching ESL reading, writing, listening and speaking and ESL testing and assessment. By the same token, the Center for English Literacy's (CEL) annual professional development seminar primarily teaches how to teach phonics, vocabulary lists and game activities. It is understandable that teachers want to learn about new and rigorous teaching methods, but at the same time, discussing the EL learners' sociocultural contexts, identity building processes, investment priorities and social responsibilities through English teaching should also be included in teacher training curricula. By doing so, we should be able to keep our students in the classroom, to help their superación and thus improve our society as a whole.

Viewing first language use as affordances than constraints

Among the many moments in the adult ELs class when they felt superación or oppressions, I would like to highlight the incidents when the teachers banned using students' first language (L1) with a social justice lens. Recall that when Domingo, Christian and Mag tried to understand the class contents and instructions by talking to each other in Spanish, the teachers said 'no Spanish, but only English'. It may be understandable to use the target language only in L2 classrooms; however, this L1 banning policy seemed to oppress the students and damage their heritage and identity just as the subtractive schooling did (Macedo, 2000; Valenzuela, 2005). Therefore, it is unjust and such incidents worked as triggering components for some students' decision to cut their investment and drop out. The teachers might have considered the students' L1 use a constraint; however, we should treat it as an affordance to transform their own capital – Spanish linguistic knowledge and network resources among classmates, to acquire new capital – gaining English linguistic knowledge via utilizing and transforming their L1 knowledge (Bourdieu, 1987; Darvin & Norton, 2015).

Visit and Listen: Teacher as an Ethnographer

Noddings (2013) argues that teachers, regardless of subject, should be ethnographers. The message was that teachers as human–human interacting agents of one's education and growth, must carefully listen to their students' voices to authentically support their learning. EL teachers in particular are required to be ethnographers even more in this sense, because EL students by nature encounter, experience and struggle with different cultural norms, identity struggles and ideology conflicts based on their multiple roles (Gunn, 2003; Norton, 1997). One simple response from teachers and administrators toward adult EL students' dropout rates is saying that 'they are busy'. Perhaps some teachers and administrators might think that 'we already know what the people need and want. Asking them is a waste of time' (Freire, 1998: 118). Unlike superfluous thoughts, this study showed that students are active agents capable of making decisions for themselves. In other words, their decision to drop out is not a situational problem, but rather an active decision because they want to invest their time and energy in something more meaningful for their superación. For example, Elsa kept saying that she would stay home, watch TV and relax rather than sit and listen to her teacher's talk, because staying home was more rewarding than going to an EL class that does not care about her superación. Whether a class is helping students' superación is not clearly measurable, but all students in this book recounted that they appreciated the approach of visiting and listening to them state their needs/expectations regarding their English learning. They also appreciated being invited to collaboratively build the curriculum. Perhaps it seems that adult EL students are struggling based on the hidden curriculum, which rarely reflects their input, both cognitively and socioculturally. Schiro's (2013: 196) point about a hidden curriculum and listening to students' sociocultural factors seems to support this need to visit, listen and reflect on students' lives in our curriculum by revealing and reforming the hidden curriculum: '...education is a social process, that the hidden curriculum has enormous influence on learners, and that all knowledge carries with it social value... they [teachers] must attend to the social, political, and moral values of the children they teach'. EL teachers should visit, listen and eventually become ethnographers to help not only their students' superación, but also their own superación.

Transforming Case Context

Throughout this book, it might be thought that the two teachers, Derek and Amy, must have done something wrong to make students drop out. However, it shows that this phenomenon seems beyond the teachers' 'faults'. Instead, it seems based on the context's bounded nature by itself. Recall that the CEL is a non-profit organization with limited funds to support teachers. Teacher Love (pseudonym, a teacher interviewed for this study) acknowledged that CEL teachers are also struggling in this context. The teachers are not full-time employees. They are assigned only two or four hours to teach per week. They have to drive to the satellite locations at night. The 'classrooms' are factory cafeterias, local library meeting rooms or local church meeting rooms. Internet access is rare. Sometimes, whiteboard and markers are not provided. Students come and go every class without any reason, and teachers are not supported in investigating further what makes the students drop out. I actually recruited three teachers to interview for this study, but two disappeared. It seems that teachers are indeed also struggling in this context, which seems to cause them to become teaching technicians who make less connections with students' real lives. Transformation for all seems necessary. Hiring full-time teachers, having a permanent building for instruction – not satellite locations, supporting teachers' further research for building rapport by visiting and listening to students and building stronger connections with students' real lives are all possible transformations.

Suggested Questionnaires for Teachers' Reflections

In everyday practice, this book shows that EL teachers should check whether their instructions improve their students' and their own superación. Based on the findings of this book, I would like to suggest a list of questions that EL teachers can use for reflecting on their instruction.

Professional development checklist for EL teachers' reflections:

- Do I care for my students?
- Do my instructions help my students improve their superación?
- Do I give them homework and check it with corrective feedback?
- Do my instructions help my students' capital gaining, identity building and ideology transformation?
- Is my instruction worth it for students to invest their time and energy? How do I know?
- Is there any support that I need from administration to help my students' superación?
- Does my instruction improve my superación?
- Did I prepare for this class?

- Is my class boring? If so, what makes it boring for my students?
- Do I just talk, talk, talk?
- Is my instruction meeting my students' expectations? How do I know?
- Is any student feeling oppressed in my class?
- Is my class topic related to my students' lives?
- Do I have dynamic activities, such as group work and presentations?
- Am I a good teacher for my students' superación?

Based on Dewey (1903) and Schiro (2013), the authentic learner-centered instruction helps self-growing not only for the students, but also for the teachers. The qualitative data in this book showed that teachers' role in retaining adult EL students seems very significant; therefore, I would urge that teachers and administrators support these reflective teacher roles in adult EL classes.

Conclusion

Language education as empowering

L2 learning is a human–human interaction. It is complex and inter-twined. Many factors connect, interact, support and sometimes contradict each other. Although the importance of this multifaceted nature of L2 learning has been discussed among scholars, it seems that the ESL research trend has been tilted to one side of SLA (e.g. cognitive aspects of learning such as how to effectively teach a specific area of language proficiency). This book would like to shed light on the importance of affective aspects when teaching an L2, because it seems that when we don't care about adult EL students, we are likely to *push* our students out of learning opportunities and self-improvement and self-actualization opportunities. Some 28 million immigrant workers in the US work in every corner of our neighborhoods while seeking help for their English learning to support their superación. We educators are not just knowledge transmitters. We are also those who will empower our students, help them raise themselves and help them transform their minds. The unheard voices and muted battles between superación and 'me no more come' are telling us to decide whether to listen to and reveal problems, and solve them, or shut our ears and eyes and continue with peripheral instruction without caring about the ecological nature of the human–human interactions. Students seem to already know the differences between just talking and real teaching. Education, especially language education is about empowering. Between giving them power or pushing them out, the choice is ours.

References

Adams, D.W. (1995) *Education for Extinction: American Indians and the Boarding School Experience, 1875–1928*. Lawrence, KS: University Press of Kansas.

Akbari, R. (2008) Transforming lives: Introducing critical pedagogy into ELT classrooms. *ELT Journal* 62 (3), 276–283.

Alicandri (2017) *Changing Terminology: From 'English Language Learners' to 'English Learners'*. Pennsylvania Department of Education. See http://www.pattan.k12.pa.us /category/Educational%20Initiatives/English%20Language%20Learners%20(ELL)/ blog/Changing_Terminology_From_English_Language_Learners_to_English_Lear ners.html

Anderson, J.R. (1995) *Learning and Memory: An Integrated Approach*. New York: Wiley.

Anyon, J. (1980) Social class and the hidden curriculum of work. *Journal of Education* 162 (1), 67–92.

Arnold, J. (2011) Attention to affect in language learning. *Online Submission* 22 (1), 11–22.

Auerbach, E.R. (1993) Reexamining English only in the ESL classroom. *TESOL Quarterly* 27 (1), 9–32.

Balfanz, R. and Fox, J. (2011) Early warning systems: Foundational research and lessons from the field. See http://www.nga.org/files/live/sites/NGA/files/pdf/1110EARLYDR OPBALFANZ.pdf

Barry-Jester, A. (2019) Latino farmworkers face serious health risks due to California's wildfires. *NBC News*. See https://www.nbcnews.com/news/latino/latino-farmworkers-face-serious-health-risks-due-california-s-wildfires-n1074691 (accessed August 15, 2021).

Barth, R.S. (1972) *Open Education and the American School*. New York: Agathon Press.

Bernat, E. (2004) Investigating Vietnamese ESL learners' beliefs about language learning. *English Australia Journal* 21 (2), 40–54.

Bernstein, B. (1971) On the classification and framing of educational knowledge. *Knowledge and Control* 3, 245–270.

Blommaert, J. (2010) *The Sociolinguistics of Globalization*. Cambridge: Cambridge University Press.

Bourdieu, P. (1977) The economics of linguistic exchanges. *Social Sciences Information* 16 (6), 645–668.

Bourdieu, P. (1984) *Distinction: A Social Critique of the Judgement of Taste*. Cambridge, MA: Harvard University Press.

Bourdieu, P. (1987) What makes a social class? On the theoretical and practical existence of groups. *Berkeley Journal of Sociology* 32, 1–17.

Brooks, N. (1975) The meaning of audiolingual. *The Modern Language Journal* 59 (5–6), 234–240.

Brown, T.S. and Perry, F.L. (1991) A comparison of three learning strategies for ESL vocabulary acquisition. *TESOL Quarterly* 25 (4), 655–670.

Bruce, M., Bridgeland, J. M., Fox, J. H. and Balfanz, R. (2011) On track for success: The use of early warning indicator and intervention systems to build a grad nation. *Civic Enterprises.*

Bruner, J.S. (1996) *The Culture of Education.* Cambridge, MA: Harvard University Press.

Bureau of Labor Statistics (2005) Chapter 6: NLS of mature and young men. In *NLS Handbook: 2005.* Washington, DC: US Department of Labour. See http://www.bls.gov/nls/handbook/2005/nlshc6.pdf (accessed December 12, 2017).

Buttaro, L. (2002) Understanding adult ESL learners: Multiple dimensions of learning and adjustments among Hispanic women. *Adult Basic Education* 11 (1), 40–61.

Buttaro, L. (2004) Second language acquisition, culture shock, and language stress of adult female Latina students in New York. *Journal of Hispanic Higher Education* 3 (1), 21–49.

Cairns, R., Cairns, B. and Neckerman, H. (1989) Early school dropout: Configurations, and determinants. *Child Development* 60, 1437–1452.

Canagarajah, A.S. (2006) TESOL at forty: What are the issues? *TESOL Quarterly* 40, 9–32.

Carraher, T.N. (1986) From drawings to buildings; working with mathematical scales. *International Journal of Behavioral Development* 9 (4), 527–544.

Carraher, T.N., Carraher, D.W. and Schliemann, A.D. (1985) Mathematics in the streets and in schools. *British Journal of Developmental Psychology* 3 (1), 21–29.

Celce-Murcia, M. (2008) Rethinking the role of communicative competence in language teaching. In E.A. Soler and M. Pilar Safont Jorda (eds) *Intercultural Language Use and Language Learning* (pp. 41–57). Dordrecht: Springer.

Center for Applied Linguistics (2021) Original Best Test. See https://www.cal.org/aea/bp/original/ (accessed September 15, 2021).

Chantrain, O.J. (2016) Complément sur la "glottophobie". *Indiscipline.* See http://indiscipline.fr/complement-sur-la-glottophobie/ (accessed December 12, 2017).

Cho, K.S. and Krashen, S.D. (1994) Acquisition of vocabulary from the Sweet Valley Kids series: Adult ESL acquisition. *Journal of Reading* 37 (8), 662–667.

Chomsky, N. (1980) Rules and representations. *Behavioral and Brain Sciences* 3 (1), 1–15.

Comings, J. (2007) Persistence: Helping adult education students reach their goals. *Review of Adult Learning and Literacy* 7 (2), 23–46.

Coney, L. (2016) The first step toward social justice: Teacher reflection. In C. Hastings and L. Jacob (eds) *Social Justice in English Language Teaching* (pp. 11–23). Alexandria, VA: TESOL Press.

Costa, P.I. and Norton, B. (2017) Introduction: Identity, transdisciplinarity, and the good language teacher. *The Modern Language Journal* 101 (S1), 3–14.

Creswell, J.W. (2012) *Qualitative Inquiry and Research Design: Choosing among Five Approaches* (3rd edn). Thousand Oaks, CA: Sage.

Cummins, J. (1994) Knowledge, power, and identity in teaching English as a second language. In F. Genesee (ed.) *Educating Second Language Children: The Whole Child, the Whole Curriculum, the Whole Community* (pp. 33–58). New York: Cambridge University Press.

Darvin, R. and Norton, B. (2015) Identity and a model of investment in applied linguistics. *Annual Review of Applied Linguistics* 35, 36–56.

DeKeyser, R. (1998) Beyond focus on form: Cognitive perspectives on learning and practicing second language grammar. In C. Doughty and J. Williams (eds) *Focus on Form in Classroom Second Language Acquisition* (pp. 42–63). New York: Cambridge University Press.

Derwing, T.M. (2003) What do ESL students say about their accents? *The Canadian Modern Language Review* 59 (4), 547–566.

Dewey, J. (1903) Democracy in education. *The Elementary School Teacher* 4, 193–204.

Doll, J.J., Eslami, Z. and Walters, L. (2013) Understanding why students drop out of high school, according to their own reports: Are they pushed or pulled, or do they fall out? A comparative analysis of seven nationally representative studies. *Sage Open* 3 (4), 1–15.

Donato, R. (1994) Collective scaffolding in second language learning. In J.P. Lantolf and G. Appel (eds) *Vygotskian Approaches to Second Language Research* (pp. 33–56). Norwood, NJ: Ablex.

Dörnyei, Z. (2005) Motivation and self-motivation. In Z. Dörnyei (ed.) *The Psychology of the Language Learner: Individual Differences in Second Language Acquisition* (pp. 65–119). Mahwah, NJ: L. Erlbaum.

Douglas Fir Group (2016) A transdisciplinary framework for SLA in a multilingual world. *Modern Language Journal* 100 (Supplement 2016), 19–47.

Dunn, W.E. and Lantolf, J.P. (1998) Vygotsky's zone of proximal development and Krashen's i+1: Incommensurable constructs; incommensurable theories. *Language Learning* 48 (3), 411–442.

Eckland, B. (1972) Explorations in Equality of Opportunity, 1955–1970: A fifteen-year follow-up study. Institute for Social Sciences Research: Chapel Hill: University of North Carolina. In Inter-university Consortium for Political and Social Research (2002) Explorations in Equality of Opportunity, 1955–1970 [United States]: A fifteen-year follow-up survey (Report No. ICPSR 7671).

Ellis, E.M. (2004) The invisible multilingual teacher: The contribution of language background to Australian ESL teachers' professional knowledge and beliefs. *International Journal of Multilingualism* 1 (2), 90–108.

Englund, M.M., Egeland, B. and Collins, W.A. (2008) Exceptions to high school dropout predictions in a low-income sample: Do adults make a difference? *Journal of Social Issues* 64 (1), 77–94.

Ennis, T.E. (1945) Jules ferry and the renaissance of French imperialism. By Thomas F. Power, Jr. *American Historical Association* 50 (2), 326–327, https://doi.org/10.1086/ahr/50.2.326.

Ensminger, M., Lamkin, R. and Jacobson, N. (1996) School leaving: A longitudinal perspective including neighborhood effects. *Child Development* 67, 2400–2416.

Fanon, F. (2008) *Black Skin, White Masks*. New York: Grove Press.

Freire, P. (1976) Literacy and the possible dream. *Prospects* 6 (1), 68–71.

Freire, P. (1996) *Pedagogy of the Oppressed* (revised). New York: Continuum.

Freire, P. (1998) *Pedagogy of Freedom: Ethics, Democracy, and Civic Courage*. Lanham, MD: Rowman & Littlefield.

Gault, T. (2003) Adult immigrant Latinas' attitudes towards ESL classes. *ITL-International Journal of Applied Linguistics* 139 (1), 101–128.

Gearing, N. and Roger, P. (2018) Ebbs and flows: A longitudinal study of an English language instructor's motivation to learn Korean. *Journal of Language, Identity & Education* 17 (5), 292–305.

Gee, J. (2012) *Situated Language and Learning: A Critique of Traditional Schooling*. New York: Routledge.

Gee, J. (2014) *Social Linguistics and Literacies: Ideology in Discourses*. Abingdon: Routledge.

Giddens, A. (1991) *Modernity and Self-Identity: Self and Society in the Late Modern Age*. Palo Alto, CA: Stanford University Press.

Gordon, D. (2004) 'I'm tired. You clean and cook'. Shifting gender identities and second language socialization. *TESOL Quarterly* 38 (3), 437–457.

Greenberg, E., Macias, R.F., Rhodes, D. and Chan, T. (2001) English literacy and language minorities in the United States (Statistical Analysis Report No. NCES2001464). Washington, DC: National Center for Educational Statistics. See https://nces.ed.gov/pubs2001/2001464_1.pdf (accessed December 12, 2017).

Griffin, L. and Alexander, K. (1978) Schooling and socioeconomic attainments: High school and college influences. *American Journal of Sociology* 84, 319–347.

Guba, E.G. and Lincoln, Y.S. (1994) Competing paradigms in qualitative research. In N.K. Denzin and Y.S. Lincoln (eds) *Handbook of Qualitative Research* (pp. 105–117). Thousand Oaks, CA: Sage Publications.

Gunn, M. (2003) Opportunity for literacy? Preliterate learners in the AMEP. *Prospect* 18 (2), 37–53.

Hall, C. (2016) A short introduction to social justice and ELT. In C. Hastings and L. Jacob (eds) *Social Justice in English Language Teaching* (pp. 3–10). Alexandria, VA: TESOL Press.

Hamp-Lyons, L. (1991) *Assessing Second Language Writing in Academic Contexts*. Norwood, NJ: Ablex Publishing Corporation.

Han, H. (2009) Institutionalized inclusion: A case study on support for immigrants in English learning. *TESOL Quarterly* 43 (4), 643–668.

Harklau, L., Losey, K.M. and Siegal, M. (eds) (1999) *Generation 1.5 Meets College Composition: Issues in the Teaching of Writing to US-Educated Learners of ESL*. New York: Routledge.

Hastings, C. and Jacob, L. (eds) (2016) *Social Justice in English Language Teaching*. Alexandria, VA: TESOL Press.

Hauser, M.D., Chomsky, N. and Fitch, W.T. (2002) The faculty of language: What is it, who has it, and how did it evolve? *Science* 298, 1569–1579.

Hopkins, J. (2002) Deaths of Hispanic workers soar 53%. *USA Today*. See https://usatoday30.usatoday.com/money/general/2002/03/25/workplace-deaths-hispanics.htm

Hsieh, Y.C. (2017) A case study of the dynamics of scaffolding among ESL learners and online resources in collaborative learning. *Computer Assisted Language Learning* 30 (1/2), 115–132. doi:10.1080/09588221.2016.1273245

Huckin, T. and Coady, J. (1999) Incidental vocabulary acquisition in a second language: A review. *Studies in Second Language Acquisition* 21 (2), 181–193.

Hyman, H.K. (2002) Foreign-accented adult ESL learners: Perceptions of their accent changes and employability qualifications. *Dissertation Abstracts International* 62 (7), 2319A.

Jianzhong, P. (2003) Colligation, collocation, and chunk in ESL vocabulary teaching and learning [J]. *Foreign Language Teaching and Research* 6, 438–445.

Jimerson, S.R., Anderson, G.E. and Whipple, A.D. (2002) Winning the battle and losing the war: Examining the relation between grade retention and dropping out of high school. *Psychology in the Schools* 39 (4), 441–457.

Jordan, W.J., Lara, J. and McPartland, J.M. (1994) *Exploring the Complexity of Early Dropout Causal Structures*. Baltimore, MD: Center for Research on Effective Schooling for Disadvantaged Students, The John Hopkins University.

Kerka, S. (2005) Learner persistence in adult basic education. *California Adult Education Research Digest* 2, 1–4.

Kim, G., Worley, C.B., Allen, R.S., Vinson, L., Crowther, M.R., Parmelee, P. and Chiriboga, D.A. (2011) Vulnerability of older Latino and Asian immigrants with limited English proficiency. *Journal of the American Geriatrics Society* 59 (7), 1246–1252.

Kim, T. (2018) 'Me no more come': Persistence and quitting among adult Spanish-speaking English learners, doctoral dissertation, University of Oklahoma.

Krapp, A. (1999) Interest, motivation and learning: An educational-psychological perspective. *European Journal of Psychology of Education* 14 (1), 23–40.

Krashen, S.D. (1982) *Child–Adult Differences in Second Language Acquisition*. Rowley, MA: Newbury House Publishers.

Lado, R. (1964) *Language Teaching: A Scientific Approach*. London: McGraw-Hill.

Lamb, M. (2004) Integrative motivation in a globalizing world. *System* 32 (1), 3–19.

Larsen-Freeman, D. (1997) Chaos/complexity science and second language acquisition. *Applied Linguistics* 18, 141–165.

Lave, J. and Wenger, E. (1991) *Situated Learning: Legitimate Peripheral Participation.* Cambridge: Cambridge University Press.

Lee, L.W. and Lu, C. (2012) 'English language learners': An analysis of perplexing ESL-related terminology. *Language and Literacy* 14 (3), 83–94.

Lightbown, P.M. and Spada, N. (2013) *How Languages are Learned* (4th edn). Oxford: Oxford University Press.

Long, M.H. (1983) Native speaker/non-native speaker conversation and the negotiation of comprehensible input. *Applied Linguistics* 4 (2), 126–141.

Long, M.H. (1996) The role of the linguistic environment in second language acquisition. In W.C. Ritchie and T.K. Bhatia (eds) *Handbook of Second Language Acquisition* (pp. 413–468). New York: Academic Press.

Macedo, D. (1994) *Literacies of Power: What Americans Are Not Allowed to Know* (expanded edn). Boulder, CO: Westview Press.

Macedo, D. (2000) The colonialism of the English only movement. *Educational Researcher* 29 (3), 15–24.

Macedo, D. and Bartolomé, L.I. (2014) Multiculturalism permitted in English only. *International Multilingual Research Journal* 8 (1), 24–37.

Mathews-Aydinli, J. (2008) Overlooked and understudied? A survey of current trends in research on adult English language learners. *Adult Education Quarterly* 58 (3), 198–213.

McKinney, C. and Norton, B. (2008) 14 identity in language and literacy education. In S. Bernard and F.M. Hult (eds) *The Handbook of Educational Linguistics* (pp. 192–205). Malden, MA: Blackwell.

McLaren, P. (2016) Critical pedagogy. In P. McLaren (ed.) *This Fist Called My Heart: The Peter McLaren Reader, Volume I* (pp. 27–66). Charlotte, NC: IAP Publishing.

McVay, R.H. (2004) Perceived barriers and factors of support for adult Mexican-American ESL students in a community college. Dissertation Abstracts International, Section A: *The Humanities and Social Sciences* 65 (5), 1632.

Menard-Warwick, J. (2005) Intergenerational trajectories and sociopolitical context: Latina immigrants in adult ESL. *TESOL Quarterly* 39 (2), 165.

National Assessment of Adult Literacy (2005) A First Look at the Literacy of America's Adults in the 21st Century. See https://nces.ed.gov/NAAL/PDF/2006470.pdf

National Center for Education Statistics (n.d) Fast facts, English language learners. See https://nces.ed.gov/fastfacts/display.asp?id=96 (accessed December 12, 2017).

Nayar, P.B. (1997) ESL/EFL dichotomy today: Language politics or pragmatics? *TESOL Quarterly* 31 (1), 9–37.

Navarez, G. (2015) Worker Deaths Decline, But Not For Latinos, Says AFL-CIO Report, *NBC News.* See http://www.nbcnews.com/news/latino/worker-deaths-decline-not-latinos-says-afl-cio-report-n350706

New England Literacy Resource Center (2009) Making It Worth the Stay. See https://nelrc.org/persist/pdfs/Making%20it%20worth%20the%20stay.pdf

Nieto, S. (1994) Moving beyond tolerance in multicultural education. *Multicultural Education* 1 (4), 9–38.

Noddings, N. (2013) *Education and Democracy in the 21st Century.* New York: Teachers College Press.

Norton, B. (1997) Language, identity, and the ownership of English. *TESOL Quarterly* 31 (3), 409–429.

Norton, B. (2012) Identity and second language acquisition. In C.A. Chapelle (ed.) *The Encyclopedia of Applied Linguistics.* Oxford: Wiley-Blackwell. https://doi.org/10.1002/9781405198431.wbeal0521.

Norton, B. and McKinney, C. (2011) An identity approach to second language learning. In D.I. Atkinson (ed.) *Alternative Approaches to Second Language Acquisition* (pp. 73–94). London: Routledge.

Norton-Peirce, B. (1995) Social identity, investment, and language learning. *TESOL Quarterly* 29 (1), 9–31.

Oklahoma State Department of Education (2015) Pre-kindergarten language screening tool for English language learners and bilingual students. See http://sde.ok.gov/sde/sites/ok.gov.sde/files/documents/files/FY16%20ELL_PreK_Screening.pdf (accessed December 12, 2017).

Oklahoma State Department of Education (2017) *Oklahoma Public Schools: Fast Facts 2016-2017*. See http://sde.ok.gov/sde/sites/ok.gov.sde/files/documents/files/Fast%20Facts%20FY17%20September%205%202017%20Update%20.pdf (accessed December 12, 2017).

Patel, L. (2015) *Decolonizing Educational Research: From Ownership to Answerability*. New York: Routledge.

Pavlenko, A. (2002) Poststructuralist approaches to the study of social factors in second language learning and use. In V. Cook (ed.) *Portraits of the L2 User* (pp. 277–302). Clevedon: Multilingual Matters.

Peirce, B.N. (1995) Social identity, investment, and language learning. *TESOL Quarterly* 29 (1), 9–31.

Peirce, B.N. (2000) *Identity and Language Learning: Gender, Ethnicity and Educational Change*. Harlow: Pearson Education.

Peirce, B.N., Harper, H. and Burnaby, B. (1993) Workplace ESL at Levi Strauss: 'dropouts' speak out. *TESL Canada Journal* 10 (2), 9–30.

Powers, R. and Wojtkiewicz, R. (2003) Occupational aspirations, gender, and educational attainment. *Sociological Spectrum* 24, 601–622.

Renninger, K. A., Hidi, S. and Krapp, A. (eds) (1992) *The Role of Interest in Learning and Development*. Mahwah, NJ: Lawrence Erlbaum Associates, Inc.

Resnick, L.B. (1987) The 1987 presidential address learning in school and out. *Educational Researcher* 16 (9), 13–54.

Richard-Amato, P.A. (1988) *Making It Happen: Interaction in the Second Language Classroom, From Theory to Practice*. White Plains, NY: Longman.

Rose, M. (2001) The working life of a waitress. *Mind, Culture & Activity* 8 (1), 3–27.

Rose, M. (2005) *The Mind at Work: Valuing the Intelligence of the American Worker*. New York: Penguin.

Rotermund, S. (2007) Why students drop out of high school: Comparisons from three national surveys (Statistical Brief No. 2). Santa Barbara, CA: California Dropout Research Project, Linguistic Minority Research Institute.

Saville-Troike, M. (1973) Reading and the audio-lingual method. *TESOL Quarterly* 7, 395–405.

Schalge, S. and Soga, K. (2008) 'Then I stop coming to school': Understanding absenteeism in an adult English as a second language program. *Adult Basic Education and Literacy Journal* 2 (3), 151–161.

Schiro, M.S. (2013) *Curriculum Theory: Conflicting Visions and Enduring Concerns*. Thousand Oaks, CA: Sage Publications.

Schmidt, R. (2001) Attention. In P. Robinson (ed.) *Cognition and Second Language Instruction* (pp. 3–32). Cambridge: Cambridge University Press.

Sesin, C. (2017) Latino farmworkers face serious health risks due to California's wildfires. *NBC News*. See https://www.nbcnews.com/news/latino/wildfires-california-s-wine-country-hit-vulnerable-immigrant-farmworkers-n809871

Shank, G.D. (2002) *Qualitative Research: A Personal Skills Approach*. Columbus, OH: Merrill Prentice Hall.

Skilton-Sylvester, E. (2002) Should I stay or should I go? Investigating Cambodian women's participation and investment in adult ESL programs. *Adult Education Quarterly* 53 (1), 9–26.

Storch, N. and Wigglesworth, G. (2003) Is there a role for the use of the L1 in an L2 setting? *TESOL Quarterly* 37 (4), 760–770. doi:10.2307/3588224

Sullivan, N. and Pratt, E. (1996) A comparative study of two ESL writing environments: A computer-assisted classroom and a traditional oral classroom. *System* 24 (4), 491–501.

Swain, M. (1995) Three functions of output in second language learning. In G. Cook and B. Seidlhofer (eds) *Principle and Practice in Applied Linguistics: Studies in Honour of HG Widdowson* (pp. 125–144). Oxford: Oxford University Press.

Swain, M. (2005) The output hypothesis: Theory and research. In E. Hinkel (ed.) *Handbook of Research in Second Language Teaching and Learning* (pp. 471–483). Mahwah, NJ: Erlbaum.

Swain, M. (2009) Languaging, agency and collaboration in advanced second language proficiency. In H. Byrnes (ed.) *Advanced Language Learning: The Contribution of Halliday and Vygotsky* (pp. 95–108). London: Continuum.

Tickle, L. (2000) *Teacher Induction: The Way Ahead*. Buckingham: Open University Press.

Tucker, J.T. (2006) The ESL logjam: Waiting times for adult ESL classes and the impact on English learners. NALEO Educational Fund.

US Census Bureau (2020) Detailed Languages Spoken at Home and Ability to Speak English for the Population 5 Years and Over: 2009-2013. See https://www.census.gov/data/tables/2013/demo/2009-2013-lang-tables.html (accessed August 15, 2021).

US Department of Education, Office of Career, Technical, and Adult Education (2010) Adult Education and Family Literacy Act of 1998, Annual Report to Congress, Program Year 2005–2006. See https://files.eric.ed.gov/fulltext/ED610073.pdf (accessed December 12, 2017).

US Department of Education, Office of Career, Technical, and Adult Education (2019) Adult Education and Family Literacy Act of 1998, Annual Report to Congress, Program Year 2015–16. See https://www2.ed.gov/about/offices/list/ovae/pi/AdultEd/aeflartc-py2015-final.pdf (accessed August 15, 2021).

US Department of Education, Office of Career, Technical, and Adult Education (2020) WIOA Statewide Performance Reports PY 2019–2020. See https://www2.ed.gov/about/offices/list/ovae/pi/AdultEd/spr/py2019/nationalsummary.pdf (accessed August 15, 2021).

US Department of Education (2021) Education Department Budget History Table: FY 1980—FY 2021 Congressional Appropriations. See https://www2.ed.gov/about/overview/budget/history/index.html (accessed August 15, 2021).

US Department of Labor (2017) News release, Bureau of Labor Statistics. Foreign-Born Workers: Labor Force Characteristics – 2016.

US Department of Labor (2021) News release, Bureau of Labor Statistics. Foreign-Born Workers: Labor Force Characteristics – 2019. See https://www.bls.gov/news.release/pdf/forbrn.pdf (accessed August 15, 2021).

Vafai, M.M. (2016) Contextualized workforce skills and ESL learner identity. *CATESOL Journal* 28 (3), 1.

Valentine, T. (1990) What motivates non-English-speaking adults to participate in the federal English-as-a-second-language program. 'Research on adult basic education' (No. 2, February 1990) Iowa: Department of Education.

Valenzuela, A. (2005) Subtractive schooling, caring relations, and social capital in the schooling of US-Mexican youth. In M. Fine and L. Weis (eds) *Beyond Silenced Voices: Class, Race, and Gender in United States Schools* (pp. 83–94). New York: State University of New York Press.

VanPatten, B. (ed.) (2004) *Processing Instruction: Theory, Research, and Commentary*. New York: Routledge.

Vinogradov, P. and Liden, A. (2009) Principled training for LESLLA instructors. *LOT Occasional Series* 15, 133–144.

Wang, D. (2006) Learn to work in a new land: The patterns and motivations for adult ESL program participation in USA. Doctoral dissertation. See https://www.proquest.com/dissertations-theses/learn-work-new-land-patterns-motivations-adult/docview/304950259/se-2?accountid=15159

Wang, A. (2016) Donald Trump plans to immediately deport 2 million to 3 million undocumented immigrants. *The Washington Post*. See https://www.washingtonpost.com/news/the-fix/wp/2016/11/13/donald-trump-plans-to-immediately-deport-2-to-3-million-undocumented-immigrants/ (accessed December 12, 2017).

Watt, D.L. and Roessingh, H. (1994) Some you win, most you lose: Tracking ESL student drop out in high school (1988–1993). *English Quarterly* 26 (3), 5–7.

Watt, D. and Roessingh, H. (2001) The dynamics of ESL drop-out: Plus ça change.... *Canadian Modern Language Review* 58 (2), 203–222.

Webster, N.L. and Lu, C. (2012) "English language learners": An analysis of perplexing ESL-related terminology. *Language and Literacy* 14 (3), 83–94.

Wenger, E. (1998) *Communities of Practice: Learning, Meaning, and Identity*. New York: Cambridge University Press.

Zhang, S. (1995) Reexamining the affective advantage of peer feedback in the ESL writing class. *Journal of Second Language Writing* 4 (3), 209–222.

About the Author

Taewoong Kim was born and raised in South Korea. He moved to the US to study second language acquisition, earning his master's in TESOL from Oklahoma City University and his PhD in Instructional Leadership and Academic Curriculum with a concentration on second language education from the University of Oklahoma. He taught ESL as well as Korean as a foreign language (KFL) for academic and community purposes. His research interests include second language acquisition, curriculum ideologies, social justice through language education, computer-assisted language learning and learner identity. He is now a lecturer at Washington University in St. Louis, MO, USA.

Index

CPSIA information can be obtained
at www.ICGtesting.com
Printed in the USA
JSHW021809090522
25754JS00003B/208

9 781800 412392